LIGHT CASSEROLES

by
Jean Paré

Dedication

The light side of comfort food.

Cover Photo

1. A Meal In One page 109
2. Chicken In Wine page 69
3. Salmon Rolls page 85

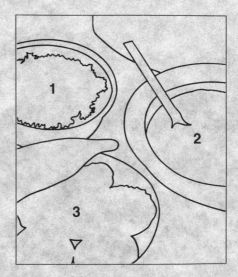

Casserole Dishes Courtesy Of:
The Bay Housewares Dept.

Serving Spoon Courtesy Of:
Le Gnome

Ceramic Dish Courtesy Of:
The Bay China Dept.

Napkin Courtesy Of:
Eaton's Linen Dept.

Vase Courtesy Of:
Whyte Clayworks Studio (1986) Ltd.

Silk Flowers Courtesy Of:
Chintz & Company

LIGHT CASSEROLES

Third Printing September 1994

I.S.B.N. 1-895455-34-0

Published and Distributed by
Company's Coming Publishing Limited
Box 8037, Station "F"
Edmonton, Alberta, Canada
T6H 4N9

**Published Simultaneously in
Canada and the United States of America**

Printed In Canada

Company's Coming Cookbooks
by Jean Paré

COMPANY'S COMING SERIES
English

HARD COVER
- JEAN PARÉ'S FAVORITES
  - Volume One

SOFT COVER
- 150 DELICIOUS SQUARES
- CASSEROLES
- MUFFINS & MORE
- SALADS
- APPETIZERS
- DESSERTS
- SOUPS & SANDWICHES
- HOLIDAY ENTERTAINING
- COOKIES
- VEGETABLES
- MAIN COURSES
- PASTA
- CAKES
- BARBECUES
- DINNERS OF THE WORLD
- LUNCHES
- PIES
- LIGHT RECIPES
- MICROWAVE COOKING
- PRESERVES
- LIGHT CASSEROLES
- CHICKEN, ETC. (April '95)

PINT SIZE BOOKS
English

SOFT COVER
- FINGER FOOD
- PARTY PLANNING
- BUFFETS
- BAKING DELIGHTS (November '94)

JEAN PARÉ LIVRES DE CUISINE
French

SOFT COVER
- 150 DÉLICIEUX CARRÉS
- LES CASSEROLES
- MUFFINS ET PLUS
- LES DÎNERS
- LES BARBECUES
- LES TARTES
- DÉLICES DES FÊTES
- RECETTES LÉGÈRES
- LES SALADES
- LA CUISSON AU MICRO-ONDES
- LES PÂTES
- LES CONSERVES
- LES CASSEROLES LÉGÈRES
- POULET, ETC. (avril '95)

table of Contents

Jean Paré was born and raised during the Great Depression in Irma, a small rural town in eastern Alberta, Canada. She grew up understanding that the combination of family, friends and home cooking is the essence of a good life. Jean learned from her mother, Ruby Elford, to appreciate good cooking and was encouraged by her father, Edward Elford, who praised even her earliest attempts. When she left home she took with her many acquired family recipes, her love of cooking and her intriguing desire to read recipe books like novels!

While raising a family of four, Jean was always busy in her kitchen preparing delicious, tasty treats and savory meals for family and friends of all ages. Her reputation flourished as the mom who would happily feed the neighborhood.

In 1963, when her children had all reached school age, Jean volunteered to cater to the 50th anniversary of the Vermilion School of Agriculture, now Lakeland College. Working out of her home, Jean prepared a dinner for over 1000 people which launched a flourishing catering operation that continued for over eighteen years. During that time she was provided with countless opportunities to test new ideas with immediate feedback – resulting in empty plates and contented customers! Whether preparing cocktail sandwiches for a house party or serving a hot meal for 1500 people, Jean Paré earned a reputation for good food, courteous service and reasonable prices.

"Why don't you write a cookbook?" Time and again, as requests for her recipes mounted, Jean was asked that question. Jean's response was to team up with her son Grant Lovig in the fall of 1980 to form Company's Coming Publishing Limited. April 14, 1981, marked the debut of "150 DELICIOUS SQUARES", the first Company's Coming cookbook in what soon would become Canada's most popular cookbook series. Jean released a new title each year for the first six years. The pace quickened and by 1987 the company had begun publishing two titles each year.

Jean Paré's operation has grown from the early days of working out of a spare bedroom in her home to operating a large and fully equipped test kitchen in Vermilion, Alberta, near the home she and her husband Larry built. Full time staff has grown steadily to include marketing personnel located in major cities across Canada plus selected U.S. markets. Home Office is located in Edmonton, Alberta where distribution, accounting and administration functions are headquartered in the company's own recently constructed 20,000 square foot facility. Company's Coming cookbooks are now distributed throughout Canada and the United States plus numerous overseas markets. Translation of the series to the Spanish and French languages began in 1990. Pint Size Books followed in 1993, offering a smaller, less expensive format focusing on more specialized topics. The recipes continued in the familiar and trusted Company's Coming style.

Jean Paré's approach to cooking has always called for quick and easy recipes using everyday ingredients. Her wonderful collection of time-honored recipes, many of which are family heirlooms, is a welcome addition to any kitchen. That's why we say: "taste the tradition".

foreword

Cooking an all-in-one dish has always been a convenient and popular way to prepare a meal. In Light Casseroles, you will find new and familiar recipes that are trimmed of calories, cholesterol, sodium and fat. Although this is not a diet or medical reference book, the recipes do contain alternative ingredients for healthy, tasty meals. When planning your daily menus, select ingredients from all food groups to ensure balanced nutrition. Choose from the many low-fat and sodium-reduced ingredients found on grocery shelves.

All recipes may be frozen before or after cooking. Allow up to twice as long if cooking from the frozen state, and be sure to use freezer-to-oven cookware.

A teflon-lined frying pan coated with no stick cooking spray is ideal for browning meats or sautéing vegetables. You will be amazed how tasty the recipes can be!

Chicken Linguini Bake is sure to please everyone at your table. Teener's Dish has always been a hit with the younger crowd. Try Tuna Divan for family or company as an easy, economical and delicious dish.

Once again, company's coming for casseroles — Light Casseroles.

Jean Paré

Today's life in the "fast lane" allows little time for cooking. Nevertheless, healthy eating and cooking are essential to a healthy lifestyle. This book on light casseroles offers many ideas of simple, one-dish meals that have ingredients from all food groups – an easy way to obtain a balance of nutrients. Other recipes can be complemented with a green salad, a roll and perhaps a glass of milk. Canned soups and vegetables are quick and handy, not necessarily unhealthy as long as they are used in moderation. The nutrition guide providing the contents of calories, cholesterol, sodium and fat for each portion or serving can help you keep things in perspective. Each recipe has been carefully analyzed using the most updated version of the Canadian Nutrient File from Health and Welfare Canada which is based upon the United States Department of Agriculture (USDA) Nutrient Data Base.

Margaret Ng, B.Sc. (Hon), M.A., R.D.
Registered Dietitian

Glossary

Calorie: A unit measure of energy which is required for healthy living. To determine the number of Calories needed to maintain the current weight of an average person, multiply the weight in pounds by 15.

	Weight	x	15 Calories	=	Average Requirement of Calories per Day
Formula					
Example	140 lbs.	x	15	=	2,100

Cholesterol: Only found in animal, fish and shellfish sources of food, not in plant foods. Guidelines for cholesterol intake generally suggest 300 mg or less per day. Cholesterol count per serving is given in each recipe to make you aware of your intake.

Egg Substitute: To use the frozen egg products on the market rather than eggs, allow one quarter cup of egg product to one large egg.

Fat: The recommended total fat intake of all foods eaten in one day should not be more than 30% of total calories, 20% is better. Be sure to include everything you eat in a day when calculating the total calories from fat. To determine the maximum fat grams for your total daily intake, the following chart will help. Remember, 1 gram of fat gives approximately 9 Calories.

Total Daily Calorie Intake	Percentage of Total Daily Calories From Fat in Grams	
	20%	30%
1200	26 grams	40 grams
1500	33 grams	50 grams
1800	40 grams	60 grams
2100	46 grams	70 grams
2400	53 grams	80 grams
2700	60 grams	90 grams
3000	66 grams	100 grams

	Total Daily Calories	x	Percent	Divide By 9	=	Total Grams Of Fat Per Day
Formula						
Example	2100	x	30%	÷ 9	=	70 g of fat

Fresh Versus Canned: Fresh food is always the wisest choice but not always the most convenient. Use canned ingredients in moderation for tasty results.

Labels: Do not be confused with % MF (milk fat) or % BF (butter fat) as seen on labels of dairy products. This percentage refers to weight of fat in the product not percentage of fat calories. For example, a cheese with 31% MF (or BF) may have 75% of its calories resulting from the fat content. Choose skim or 1% milk and low-fat dairy products.

New Products: There are new products showing up on grocery-store shelves everyday. Watch for alternatives which help you reduce your fat and sodium intake. Learn how to read manufacturer's labels so you can make wise nutritional choices.

Pepper: A pepper grinder is a great utensil. Fresh pepper will perk up any food which is on the bland side without jeopardizing the nutritional value.

Salt and Sodium: It is recommended to limit the intake of sodium to between 2000 and 3000 mg per day. Sodium is abundant in packaged and processed foods. Salt consists of 40% sodium. A teaspoon (5 mL) of salt has approximately 2000 mg of sodium. Sodium is also found in a variety of foods including dairy products, meat, poultry and vegetables. If conscientious about your sodium intake, watch for sodium-reduced versions of packaged foods, omit salt or use a salt alternative.

Salt Alternatives: Use sodium-free herbs and spices to enhance flavors of foods. For fish, try a sprinkle of basil, dill, curry or tarragon. For fruit, try allspice, cinnamon, ginger or nutmeg. For meat or poultry, cook with bay leaf, chili powder, curry, garlic, oregano, basil, thyme, hot pepper sauce, cayenne pepper or wine. For salads and vegetables, try freshly ground pepper, basil, celery seed, chives, dill, garlic, oregano, tarragon, thyme or fresh lemon juice.

Servings: As a guide to determine servings of meat, a rule of thumb is to use 4 oz. (113 g) of boneless fresh meat per person, which equals 3 oz. (84 g) of cooked meat. This is approximately the size of a deck of playing cards. A kitchen scale is a big asset.

Soup: Canned soups are wonderful convenience foods for using in preparation of many recipes. If you are on a sodium restricted diet, substitute traditional canned soups with the lower-sodium soups. There are also fat reduced soups available. Ask your grocer.

Sweetener: A liquid sugar substitute has been used for testing some of the recipes in this book. Sugar may be used if you prefer. However, to create the same degree of sweetness you will need to use about 4 times more sugar than the substitute. Total calories will also increase. One teaspoon (5 mL) of sugar has 15 Calories.

GREEN PEPPER STEAK

The tomato and green pepper adds color to this tasty dish.

Lean boneless round steak, cut into thin strips	1½ lbs.	680 g
Condensed onion soup	10 oz.	284 mL
Canned tomatoes	14 oz.	398 mL
Thinly sliced onion	½ cup	125mL
Large green pepper, seeded, cut in thin strips	1	1
Sliced fresh mushrooms	2 cups	500 mL
Light soy sauce (40% less salt)	1 tbsp.	15 mL
Pepper	⅛ tsp.	0.5 mL

Spray frying pan with no-stick cooking spray. Add steak strips. Sauté until browned. Turn into 2 quart (2 L) casserole.

Stir remaining ingredients together in bowl. Pour over meat. Stir. Cover. Bake in 350°F (175°C) oven for 1½ to 2 hours until very tender. Makes 5 cups (1.13 L).

Pictured on page 71.

NUTRITION GUIDE	1 cup (225 mL) contains:	
	Energy	221 Calories (924 kJ)
	Cholesterol	63 mg
	Sodium	808 mg
	Fat	6 g

BURGER SPROUT SPECIAL

Let the good times roll. This will be ready for the finale.

Lean ground beef	1 lb.	454 g
Chopped onion	2 cups	500 mL
Sliced celery	1 cup	250 mL
Long grain rice, uncooked	½ cup	125 mL
Fresh bean sprouts, packed	2 cups	500 mL
Condensed cream of mushroom soup	2 × 10 oz.	2 × 284 mL
Water	1½ cups	375 mL
Light soy sauce (40% less salt)	3 tbsp.	50 mL
Pepper	¼ tsp.	1 mL

(continued on next page)

Spray frying pan with no-stick cooking spray. Add ground beef. Scramble-fry to brown. Transfer to 3 quart (3 L) casserole.

Add next 4 ingredients. Stir.

Combine remaining 4 ingredients in bowl. Stir until smooth. Pour over top. Stir lightly. Cover. Bake in 350°F (175°C) oven for 1¼ hours. Stir. Bake, uncovered, for 15 minutes more until rice is cooked. Makes 7⅓ cups (1.65 L).

N U T R I T I O N G U I D E	1 cup (225 mL) contains:	
	Energy	251 Calories (1051 kJ)
	Cholesterol	33 mg
	Sodium	967 mg
	Fat	11.5 g

RUSTIC MEATLOAF

A mixture of beef and turkey makes up this good loaf. Good choice.

Lean ground beef	¾ lb.	375 g
Ground skinless turkey breast	¾ lb.	375 g
Finely chopped onion	¾ cup	175 mL
Dry bread crumbs	⅓ cup	75 mL
Water	⅓ cup	75 mL
Ketchup, page 99	⅓ cup	75 mL
Large egg, beaten	1	1
Light soy sauce (40% less salt)	2 tbsp.	30 mL
Beef bouillon powder (35% less salt)	1 tsp.	5 mL
Pepper	¼ tsp.	1 mL
Garlic powder	¼ tsp.	1 mL
Gravy browner	¼ tsp.	1 mL

Mix first 11 ingredients in large bowl. Shape into loaf about 8 x 4 inches (20 x 10 cm). Place on foil lined baking sheet. Bake, uncovered, in 350°F (175°C) oven for about 1 hour.

Using damp brush, dip in gravy browner and brush over loaf before serving. Makes 8 servings.

N U T R I T I O N G U I D E	1 serving contains:	
	Energy	170 Calories (710 kJ)
	Cholesterol	81 mg
	Sodium	347 mg
	Fat	5 g

BAKED CHOP SUEY

The no-fuss way to do this dish.

Boneless sirloin steak, fat removed, cut in short thin strips	1 lb.	454 g
Chopped onion	1 cup	250 mL
Chopped celery	1 cup	250 mL
Fresh bean sprouts, packed	2 cups	500 mL
Sliced fresh mushrooms	2 cups	500 mL
Condensed cream of mushroom soup	10 oz.	284 mL
Grated low-fat sharp Cheddar cheese (less than 21% MF)	½ cup	125 mL
Chow mein noodles	⅓ cup	75 mL
Red pepper rings, for garnish		

Spray frying pan with no-stick cooking spray. Add steak strips. Sauté until browned.

Stir in next 5 ingredients. Turn into 2 quart (2 L) casserole. It will be quite full but will cook down. Cover. Bake in 350°F (175°C) oven for 60 minutes or until meat is tender.

Sprinkle with cheese and noodles. Arrange pepper rings down center. Bake, uncovered, about 15 minutes more. Makes 5 servings.

Pictured on page 35.

NUTRITION GUIDE	1 serving contains:	
	Energy	259 Calories (1083 kJ)
	Cholesterol	50 mg
	Sodium	648 mg
	Fat	11.5 g

Did you hear about the glass blower who inhaled? He had a pane in his stomach.

Add a green salad and you're ready.

Lean round steak	**1 lb.**	**454 g**
Salt, sprinkle (optional)		
Pepper, sprinkle		
Paprika, sprinkle		
Sliced onion	**1 cup**	**250 mL**
Frozen cut green beans	**2 cups**	**500 mL**
Peeled, sliced potato	**3 cups**	**750 mL**
Canned tomatoes, mashed	**1 cup**	**250 mL**
Ketchup, page 99	**1 tbsp.**	**15 mL**
Salt	**¹/₂ tsp.**	**2 mL**
Granulated sugar	**¹/₂ tsp.**	**2 mL**

Spray frying pan with no-stick cooking spray. Add steak. Brown both sides well. Sprinkle with salt, pepper and paprika. Cut into 4 pieces. Place in 3 quart (3 L) casserole.

Add onion layer, then beans and potato.

Place next 4 ingredients in frying pan. Stir to loosen brown bits. Pour into casserole. Cover. Bake in 350°F (175°C) oven for 1³/₄ to 2 hours until meat is tender. Add a bit of water if it dries. Makes 4 servings.

NUTRITION GUIDE	1 serving contains:	
	Energy	276 Calories (1155 kJ)
	Cholesterol	53 mg
	Sodium	519 mg
	Fat	4.7 g

Paré Pointer

Television has opened many doors, mostly refrigerator.

CROWD PLEASING CHILI

So simple to increase to feed large numbers. Chili powder may be increased to suit your taste.

Lean ground beef	1 lb.	454 g
Chopped onion	1¼ cups	275 mL
Chopped celery	1¼ cups	275 mL
Chopped green pepper	1 cup	250 mL
Diced fresh tomatoes (see Note)	2½ cups	575 mL
Condensed tomato soup	10 oz.	284 mL
Kidney beans with juice	14 oz.	398 mL
Chili powder	1 tsp.	5 mL
Prepared mustard	1 tsp.	5 mL
Pepper	¼ tsp.	1 mL
Granulated sugar	1 tsp.	5 mL

Spray large Dutch oven with no-stick cooking spray. Add ground beef. Brown, stirring often to break up.

Add remaining ingredients. Stir. Bring to a boil. Simmer, covered, for about 30 minutes to cook vegetables and to blend flavors. Makes 6⅔ cups (1.5 L).

Pictured on page 71.

N U T R I T I O N G U I D E	1 cup (225 mL) contains:	
	Energy	224 Calories (936 kJ)
	Cholesterol	35 mg
	Sodium	604 mg
	Fat	7 g

Note: One 14 oz. (398 mL) can of tomatoes can be substituted for fresh tomatoes, but sodium content will be higher.

Paré Pointer

The son told his dad he was quitting his studies to drive big machinery. His dad said he wouldn't stand in his way.

QUICK TAMALE CASSEROLE

Get the tamale flavor the easy way.

Lean ground beef	1 lb.	454 g
Chopped onion	1 cup	250 mL
Canned tomatoes	14 oz.	398 mL
Yellow cornmeal	½ cup	125 mL
Kernel corn, fresh or frozen	1½ cups	325 mL
Chili powder	1 tsp.	5 mL
Salt	½ tsp.	2 mL
Pepper	¼ tsp.	1 mL

Spray frying pan with no-stick cooking spray. Add ground beef and onion. Sauté until onions are soft and no pink remains in meat. Remove from heat.

Combine tomatoes and cornmeal in saucepan. Bring to a boil and simmer for 5 minutes, stirring occasionally.

Add remaining ingredients along with meat mixture. Stir. Turn into 2 quart (2 L) casserole. Bake, uncovered, in 350°F (175°C) oven for about 30 minutes. Makes 6 servings.

Pictured on page 53.

N U T R I T I O N
G U I D E

1 serving contains:

Energy	223 Calories (934 kJ)
Cholesterol	39 mg
Sodium	376 mg
Fat	7 g

Pâré Pointer

Steady. Try not to lose your grip. Especially when you are catching a train.

STEWED BEEF CHUNKS

Tender beef in a rich brown gravy.

Lean beef stew meat	**2 lbs.**	**900 g**
Onion flakes	**3 tbsp.**	**50 mL**
Beef bouillon powder (35% less salt)	**1 tbsp.**	**15 mL**
Condensed golden mushroom soup	**10 oz.**	**284 mL**
Sherry (or alcohol-free sherry)	**½ cup**	**125 mL**

Lay meat in small roaster.

In small bowl, stir onion flakes, bouillon powder, soup and sherry together well. Pour over meat. Cover. Bake in 325°F (160°C) oven for 2½ to 3 hours until tender. Makes 8 servings.

NUTRITION GUIDE	**1 serving contains:**	
	Energy	140 Calories (585 kJ)
	Cholesterol	46 mg
	Sodium	436 mg
	Fat	4.4 g

1. Bannock Biscuits Modern page 100
2. Potato Biscuits page 102
3. Oriental Tuna Casserole page 83
4. Wiener Pasta Bake page 124
5. Ham Rolls page 129

Pasta is added raw to this casserole. A real time saver in preparation.

Lean ground beef	1 lb.	454 g
Chopped onion	1 cup	250 mL
Green pepper, seeded and slivered	1	1
Frozen kernel corn	1½ cups	375 mL
Salt	¾ tsp.	4 mL
Pepper	¼ tsp.	1 mL
Dry colored fusilli (or other pasta)	2⅔ cups	600 mL
Tomato juice	2¾ cups	675 mL
Grated low-fat sharp Cheddar cheese (less than 21% MF)	1 cup	250 mL

Spray frying pan with no-stick cooking spray. Add ground beef, onion and green pepper. Sauté until no pink remains in meat and onion is soft.

Add corn, salt and pepper. Stir.

Layer ½ dry fusilli in 3 quart (3 L) casserole followed by ½ meat mixture, second ½ fusilli and second ½ meat.

Pour tomato juice over all. Cover. Bake in 350°F (175°C) oven for about 1 hour 25 minutes until noodles are tender.

Sprinkle with cheese. Bake, uncovered, for 5 minutes more. Makes 6⅔ cups (1.5 L).

Pictured on page 125.

Pictured on page 125.

NUTRITION GUIDE	1 cup (225 mL) contains:	
	Energy	351 Calories (1468 kJ)
	Cholesterol	46 mg
	Sodium	820 mg
	Fat	9.5 g

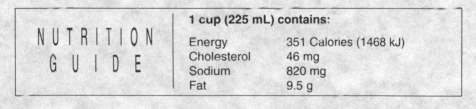

PORCUPINES

Carrot and green pepper sticks make this a colorful casserole.

Lean ground beef	1 lb.	454 g
Long grain rice, uncooked	½ cup	125 mL
Finely chopped onion	¼ cup	50 mL
Salt	½ tsp.	2 mL
Pepper	¼ tsp.	1 mL
Sliced onion	1 cup	250 mL
Green pepper, seeded, cut in strips	½	½
Strips of carrot	½ cup	125 mL
Tomato juice	3 cups	750 mL

Put first 5 ingredients in bowl. Mix. Shape into 25 balls. Arrange in 9 x 9 inch (22 x 22 cm) pan, or 3 quart (3 L) casserole, in single layer.

Lay onion slices, green pepper strips and carrot strips among meatballs.

Pour tomato juice over top. Cover. Bake in 350°F (175°C) oven for about 1 hour until rice is cooked. Makes 25 meatballs.

Pictured on page 143.

N U T R I T I O N G U I D E	**1 meatball contains:**	
	Energy	49 Calories (206 kJ)
	Cholesterol	9 mg
	Sodium	172 mg
	Fat	1.5 g

Experience enables you to recognize a mistake when you make it again.

Similar to an extra-meaty lazy cabbage roll casserole.

Small head of cabbage, coarsely grated	**1½ lbs.**	**680 g**
Dry elbow macaroni	**½ cup**	**125 mL**
Lean ground beef	**1 lb.**	**454 g**
Chopped onion	**1 cup**	**250 mL**
Salt	**½ tsp.**	**2 mL**
Pepper	**¼ tsp.**	**1 mL**
Condensed tomato soup	**10 oz.**	**284 mL**
Water	**1 cup**	**250 mL**

Layer ½ cabbage in 2 quart (2 L) casserole. Spread macaroni over top.

Spray frying pan with no-stick cooking spray. Add ground beef, onion, salt and pepper. Scramble-fry until brown and onion is soft. Layer over macaroni. Add second layer of cabbage over top.

Stir soup and water together in small bowl. Pour over all. Do not stir. Cover. Bake in 350°F (175°C) oven for 1 to 1½ hours until cabbage and macaroni are tender. Makes 6 servings.

NUTRITION GUIDE	1 serving contains:	
	Energy	229 Calories (959 kJ)
	Cholesterol	39 mg
	Sodium	635 mg
	Fat	7.6 g

When the grape got stepped on it didn't cry out. It just let out a wine.

BEEFY CHEESE BAKE

With low-fat yogurt and cream cheese, you're way ahead on fat savings with this good casserole.

Dry tiny shells (or other pasta)	2 cups	500 mL
Boiling water	3 qts.	3 L
Lean ground beef	1 lb.	454 g
Canned tomatoes, mashed	14 oz.	398 mL
Salt	$\frac{1}{2}$ tsp.	2 mL
Garlic powder (or 2 cloves minced)	$\frac{1}{4}$ tsp.	1 mL
Granulated sugar	$\frac{1}{2}$ tsp.	2 mL
Low-fat plain yogurt (less than 1% MF)	1 cup	250 mL
All-purpose flour	2 tbsp.	30 mL
Low-fat cream cheese (less than 20% MF), softened	4 oz.	125 g
Green onions, sliced	6	6
Grated low-fat sharp Cheddar cheese (less than 21% MF)	$\frac{1}{2}$ cup	125 mL

Cook shells in boiling water in large uncovered pot about 8 to 11 minutes, until tender but firm. Drain. Pour into 3 quart (3 L) casserole.

Scramble-fry ground beef in frying pan that has been sprayed with no-stick cooking spray, until no pink remains in meat.

Add tomatoes, salt, garlic powder and sugar. Stir. Pour over pasta shells.

Stir yogurt and flour together well in bowl. Add cream cheese. Mash together. Stir in onion. Spoon over meat layer.

Bake, uncovered, in 350°F (175°C) oven for 25 minutes. Sprinkle with cheese. Continue to bake for about 5 minutes more. Makes 7$\frac{3}{4}$ cups (1.74 L).

NUTRITION GUIDE	1 cup (225 mL) contains:	
	Energy	275 Calories (1149 kJ)
	Cholesterol	46 mg
	Sodium	469 mg
	Fat	8 g

SWEET AND SOUR MEATBALLS

Sugar-free grape jelly is used to make this good sauce. Make meatballs smaller to use as an appetizer.

MEATBALLS

Dry bread crumbs	½ cup	125 mL
All-purpose flour	2 tbsp.	30 mL
Salt	½ tsp.	2 mL
Pepper	¼ tsp.	1 mL
Garlic powder	¼ tsp.	1 mL
Parsley flakes	½ tsp.	2 mL
Water	½ cup	125 mL
Finely chopped onion	⅓ cup	75 mL
Lean ground beef	1 lb.	454 g

SWEET AND SOUR SAUCE

Boiling water	1 cup	250 mL
Low-calorie grape jelly	½ cup	125 mL
Ketchup, page 99	¼ cup	60 mL
Cornstarch	2 tbsp.	30 mL
Water	2 tbsp.	30 mL

Meatballs: Combine first 8 ingredients in bowl. Stir well.

Add ground beef. Mix. Shape into 30 balls. Arrange on baking sheet with sides. Cook in 375°F (190°C) oven for 15 to 20 minutes.

Sweet And Sour Sauce: Stir boiling water and jelly together in saucepan. Add ketchup. Stir. Bring to a boil stirring occasionally.

Mix cornstarch and second amount of water together in small cup. Stir into boiling liquid until it boils and thickens. Pour over meatballs. Cover. Bake in 350°F (175°C) oven for 20 minutes or until hot. Makes 30 meatballs with 1¼ cups (275 mL) sauce.

NUTRITION GUIDE	1 meatball with 2 tsp. (10 mL) sauce contains:	
	Energy	42 Calories (175 kJ)
	Cholesterol	8 mg
	Sodium	80 mg
	Fat	1.4 g

MOCK RAVIOLI

A simple way to make ravioli. The pasta layers are sandwiched with a dark vegetable-meat filling. Just spicy enough.

Frozen chopped spinach	2 x 10 oz.	2 x 284 g
Sliced fresh mushrooms	2 cups	500 mL
Canned tomatoes, mashed	28 oz.	796 mL
Chopped onion	3 cups	750 mL
Parsley flakes	1 tsp.	5 mL
Ground rosemary	1 tsp.	5 mL
Thyme	1 tsp.	5 mL
Oregano	1 tsp.	5 mL
Granulated sugar	1 tsp.	5 mL
Lean ground beef	1 lb.	454 g
Salt	½ tsp.	2 mL
Pepper	¼ tsp.	1 mL
Garlic powder	¼ tsp.	1 mL
Lasagne noodles	9	9
Boiling water	4 qts.	4 L
Grated low-fat sharp Cheddar cheese (less than 21% MF)	1 cup	250 mL

Combine first 9 ingredients in large saucepan. Bring to a boil. Simmer about 30 minutes, stirring occasionally.

Spray frying pan with no-stick cooking spray. Add ground beef. Brown well, breaking up chunks. Add salt, pepper and garlic powder. Stir into spinach mixture.

In large uncovered Dutch oven, cook noodles in boiling water until tender but firm, about 14 to 16 minutes. Drain. Rinse with cold water. Drain. Line bottom of 9 x 13 inch (22 x 33 cm) pan with 3 long noodles. Spread ⅓ meat mixture over top. Repeat twice. Bake, uncovered, in 350°F (175°C) oven for about 20 minutes until hot.

Sprinkle with cheese. Bake for 5 minutes more. Cuts into 12 pieces.

NUTRITION GUIDE	1 piece contains:	
	Energy	194 Calories (814 kJ)
	Cholesterol	25 mg
	Sodium	344 mg
	Fat	6 g

Once this is in the oven, your mind will be at ease. One-pot cooking at its best.

Beef roast, fat removed, cheaper cut	3 lbs.	1.36 kg
Water	1 cup	250 mL
Medium potatoes, peeled and quartered	6	6
Medium carrots, halved	12	12
Medium onions, quartered	4	4
Celery ribs, quartered	6	6

Place beef in roaster. Add water. Cover. Bake in 300°F (150°C) oven for 2½ hours.

Pile all 4 vegetables around meat. Cover. Continue to bake for about 1¼ hours or until vegetables are tender. Remove vegetables and keep warm while you make gravy if desired. Makes 12 servings.

NUTRITION GUIDE	1 serving contains:	
	Energy	251 Calories (1051 kJ)
	Cholesterol	45 mg
	Sodium	124 mg
	Fat	4 g

GRAVY

Juice left in roaster plus water to make	2 cups	500 mL
All-purpose flour	¼ cup	60 mL
Water	¼ cup	60 mL
Beef bouillon powder (35% less salt)	2 tsp.	10 mL
Pepper	⅛ tsp.	0.5 mL
Gravy browning sauce, if needed		

Gravy: Juice may be left in roaster or poured into smaller saucepan. Bring to a boil.

Mix flour with second amount of water until no lumps remain. Stir into boiling liquid, along with remaining ingredients, until it boils and thickens. Add more water to thin if desired. Makes 2 cups (450 mL).

NUTRITION GUIDE	2 tbsp. (30 mL) contains:	
	Energy	9 Calories (37 kJ)
	Cholesterol	trace
	Sodium	39 mg
	Fat	trace

BEANS AND MEATBALL DISH

A great team. Meatballs are covered with beans followed by a tasty sauce. Dark and delicious.

Large egg	1	1
Skim milk	½ cup	125 mL
Regular or quick rolled oats (not instant)	½ cup	125 mL
Salt	½ tsp.	2 mL
Pepper	¼ tsp	1 mL
Lean ground beef	1 lb.	454 g
Canned beans in tomato sauce	14 oz.	398 mL
Chopped onions	1 cup	250 mL
Water		
Ketchup, page 99	½ cup	125 mL
White vinegar	2 tbsp.	30 mL
Worcestershire sauce	1 tbsp.	15 mL
Liquid sweetener (or 2 tbsp., 30 mL, brown sugar)	1½ tsp.	7 mL

Beat egg in bowl. Add milk, rolled oats, salt and pepper. Stir.

Mix in ground beef. Shape into 20 meatballs. Arrange on baking sheet with sides. Bake in 375°F (190°C) oven for 20 minutes. Turn into 3 quart (3 L) casserole in single layer.

Spoon beans over meatballs.

Cook onion in some water until tender. Drain.

Add remaining ingredients to onion. Stir. Pour over beans. Bake, uncovered, in 350°F (175°F) oven for 20 to 30 minutes until hot and bubbly. Makes 8 servings.

NUTRITION GUIDE	1 serving contains:	
	Energy	205 Calories (858 kJ)
	Cholesterol	60 mg
	Sodium	587 mg
	Fat	6.3 g

TOMATO NOODLE CASSEROLE

Layers of noodles and meat with melted cheese on top. Family size without the richer fat content of regular cheese.

Dry fettuccine	8 oz.	250 g
Boiling water	3 qts.	3 L
Chopped onion	1 cup	250 mL
Lean ground beef	1 lb.	454 g
Canned tomatoes, mashed	2 × 14 oz.	2 × 398 mL
Oregano	2 tsp.	10 mL
Granulated sugar	1 tsp.	5 mL
Salt	1 tsp.	5 mL
Grated part-skim mozzarella cheese (35% less fat)	2 cups	500 mL

Cook fettuccine in boiling water in large uncovered saucepan about 9 to 11 minutes until tender but firm. Drain. Pour into 3 quart (3 L) casserole.

Spray frying pan with no-stick cooking spray. Add onion and ground beef. Scramble-fry until brown and onion is soft.

Add tomatoes, oregano, sugar, and salt. Stir. Pour over fettuccine. Bake, uncovered, in 350°F (175°C) oven for 30 minutes.

Sprinkle cheese over top. Bake for 5 to 10 minutes more until cheese melts. Makes 8½ cups (1.91 L).

NUTRITION GUIDE	1 cup (225 mL) contains:	
	Energy	294 Calories (1230 kJ)
	Cholesterol	44 mg
	Sodium	631 mg
	Fat	9.7 g

PATTIES IN GRAVY

This has lots of gravy to serve over rice or mashed potatoes.

PATTIES

Dry bread crumbs	²/₃ **cup**	**150 mL**
All-purpose flour	**2 tbsp.**	**30 mL**
Allspice	**1 tsp.**	**5 mL**
Pepper	¹/₄ **tsp.**	**1 mL**
Skim milk	¹/₂ **cup**	**125 mL**
Lean ground beef	**1 lb.**	**454 g**

GRAVY

Condensed tomato soup	**10 oz.**	**284 mL**
Beef bouillon powder (35% less salt)	**2 tsp.**	**10 mL**
Onion flakes	**2 tbsp.**	**30 mL**
Water	**1¹/₄ cups**	**275 mL**

Patties: Combine first 4 ingredients in bowl. Stir.

Mix in milk, then ground beef. Shape into 8 patties. Brown both sides under broiler. Turn into 2 quart (2 L) casserole.

Gravy: Stir all 4 ingredients together. Pour over patties. Cover. Bake in 350°F (175°C) oven for about 1 hour. Makes 8 patties and 1²/₃ cups (375 mL) gravy.

NUTRITION GUIDE	**1 patty plus 3¹/₃ tbsp. (50 mL) gravy contains:**	
	Energy	166 Calories (695 kJ)
	Cholesterol	30 mg
	Sodium	428 mg
	Fat	5.8 g

A doctor tries hard to keep his temper. He doesn't want to lose patients.

Carrots and celery add color as does the gravy. An economical way to serve steak.

Lean boneless round steak, fat removed, cut in 8 pieces	2 lbs.	900 g
All-purpose flour	¼ cup	60 mL
Water	1½ cups	375 mL
Canned tomatoes	14 oz.	398 mL
Chopped onion	1 cup	250 mL
Sliced celery	¾ cup	175 mL
Sliced carrots	¾ cup	175 mL
Salt	1 tsp.	5 mL
Pepper	¼ tsp.	1 mL

Spray frying pan with no-stick cooking spray. Add steak. Brown both sides. Transfer to small roaster or 3 quart (3 L) casserole.

Place flour in small bowl. Add water gradually, mixing until no lumps remain. Pour into frying pan. Stir, loosening brown bits, until it boils and thickens.

Add remaining ingredients. Stir. Pour over steak. Cover. Bake in 350°F (175°C) oven for about 1½ to 2 hours until meat is tender. Makes 8 servings.

NUTRITION GUIDE	1 serving contains:	
	Energy	171 Calories (715 kJ)
	Cholesterol	52 mg
	Sodium	470 mg
	Fat	4.4 g

The best way to eat a grapefruit is by yourself.

SWISS STEAK

Served with good brown gravy. A slight hint of horseradish.

Boneless round steak, fat removed, cut into 8 pieces	2 lbs.	900 g
All-purpose flour	¼ cup	60 mL
Water	2 cups	450 mL
Sliced onion	2 cups	500 mL
Low-fat plain yogurt (less than 1% MF)	½ cup	125 mL
Prepared horseradish	1 tbsp.	15 mL
Salt	½ tsp.	2 mL
Pepper	¼ tsp.	1 mL
Paprika	⅛ tsp.	0.5 mL

Spray frying pan with no-stick cooking spray. Add steak. Brown both sides. Transfer to 3 quart (3 L) casserole.

Place flour in small bowl. Add water gradually, mixing until no lumps remain. Pour into frying pan, stirring until it boils and thickens. Loosen all brown bits in pan.

Stir in remaining ingredients. Pour over steak. Cover. Bake in 350°F (175°C) oven for 1½ to 2 hours until meat is fork tender. Makes 8 servings.

N U T R I T I O N G U I D E	1 serving contains:	
	Energy	171 Calories (714 kJ)
	Cholesterol	53 mg
	Sodium	219 mg
	Fat	4.3 g

Paré Pointer

A piano and a fish are quite different. You can't tuna fish.

Pretty as a picture. Mild flavored. Excellent choice.

Lean ground beef	1 lb.	454 g
Tomato sauce	7½ oz.	213 mL
Dry colored fusilli (or other pasta)	2⅔ cup	600 mL
Boiling water	2½ qts.	3 L
Low-fat cottage cheese (less than 1% MF)	1 cup	250 mL
Low-fat plain yogurt (less than 1% MF)	1 cup	250 mL
All-purpose flour	2 tbsp.	30 mL
Green onions, chopped	6	6
Salt	½ tsp.	2 mL
Pepper	⅛ tsp.	0.5 mL
Garlic powder	¼ tsp.	1 mL
Grated low-fat sharp Cheddar cheese (less than 21% MF)	¼ cup	60 mL

Scramble-fry ground beef in frying pan that has been sprayed with no-stick cooking spray.

Add tomato sauce. Stir. Simmer 5 minutes.

In large uncovered saucepan, cook fusilli in boiling water about 8 minutes until tender but firm. Drain.

Add next 7 ingredients to pasta. Stir well. Using 2 quart (2 L) casserole, alternate 2 layers of beef mixture with 2 layers pasta, making beef the first layer. Bake, uncovered, in 350°F (175°C) oven for about 30 minutes until hot.

Sprinkle with cheese. Bake about 5 minutes more or until cheese is melted. Makes 6¾ cups (1.53 L).

NUTRITION GUIDE	1 cup (225 mL) contains:	
	Energy	324 Calories (1354 kJ)
	Cholesterol	42 mg
	Sodium	663 mg
	Fat	8 g

SAUERKRAUT CASSEROLE

With a shiny golden topping. Includes meat and potatoes.

Potatoes, peeled and quartered	**2 lbs.**	**900 g**
Water		
Lean ground beef	**1½ lbs.**	**680 g**
Finely chopped onion	**½ cup**	**125 mL**
White vinegar	**3 tbsp.**	**50 mL**
Chili powder	**1 tbsp.**	**15 mL**
Oregano	**1 tsp.**	**5 mL**
Salt	**½ tsp.**	**2 mL**
Pepper	**¼ tsp.**	**1 mL**
Garlic powder	**¼ tsp.**	**1 mL**
Water	**¼ cup**	**50 mL**
Sauerkraut, rinsed and drained	**28 oz.**	**796 mL**
Grated Parmesan cheese	**1½ tbsp.**	**25 mL**

Cook potatoes in some water until tender. Drain. Mash.

Spray frying pan with no-stick cooking spray. Add ground beef and onion. Scramble-fry until no pink remains in meat.

Add next 7 ingredients. Stir.

Spread sauerkraut in bottom of 3 quart (3 L) casserole. Cover with meat mixture. Place potato over top. Smooth.

Sprinkle with Parmesan cheese. Bake, uncovered, in 350°F (175°C) oven for about 35 minutes. Makes 8¾ cups (2 L).

NUTRITION GUIDE	1 cup (225 mL) contains:	
	Energy	236 Calories (986 kJ)
	Cholesterol	41 mg
	Sodium	635 mg
	Fat	7.1 g

Soft and moist.

Tomato sauce	7½ oz.	213 mL
Corn syrup	¼ cup	60 mL
Prepared mustard	2 tbsp.	30 mL
Egg whites (large)	2	2
Finely chopped peeled apple	1 cup	250 mL
Chopped onion	½ cup	125 mL
Tomato mixture		
Fine dry bread crumbs	¾ cup	175 mL
Worcestershire sauce	1 tsp.	5 mL
Salt	1 tsp.	5 mL
Nutmeg	½ tsp.	2 mL
Pepper	⅛ tsp.	0.5 mL
Lean ground beef	1½ lbs.	680 g
Reserved tomato mixture	3 tbsp.	50 mL

In small bowl stir tomato sauce, corn syrup and mustard. Measure and reserve 3 tbsp. (50 mL) for topping.

Beat egg whites with spoon in large bowl. Add next 8 ingredients. Stir well.

Mix in ground beef. Turn into 9 x 5 inch (23 x 12 cm) loaf pan which has been sprayed with no-stick cooking spray. Cook, uncovered, in 350°F (175°C) oven for 1 hour.

Smooth reserved tomato mixture over top. Continue to cook for about 15 minutes more. Let stand 10 minutes before cutting into 10 slices.

N U T R I T I O N
G U I D E

1 slice contains:

Energy	185 Calories (775 kJ)
Cholesterol	35 mg
Sodium	553 mg
Fat	6.3 g

SHIPWRECK WITH BEANS

A full meal with the addition of kidney beans for extra protein without added fat.

Chopped onions	3 cups	750 mL
Lean ground beef	1 lb.	454 g
Kidney beans with juice	14 oz.	398 mL
Chopped celery	1½ cups	375 mL
Long grain rice, uncooked	½ cup	125 mL
Medium potatoes, peeled and sliced	2	2
Condensed tomato soup	10 oz.	284 mL
Hot water	1¼ cups	275 mL

Layer first 6 ingredients in 3 quart (3 L) casserole in order given.

Stir soup and water together well. Pour over all. Cover. Bake in 350°F (175°C) oven for 2 to 2½ hours until vegetables are tender. Makes 9¼ cups (2 L).

N U T R I T I O N G U I D E	1 cup (225 mL) contains:	
	Energy	222 Calories (931 kJ)
	Cholesterol	25 mg
	Sodium	425 mg
	Fat	4.9 g

1. Special Day Ribs page 128
2. Shrimp Creole page 92
3. Brandied Fruit page 102
4. Baked Chop Suey page 12

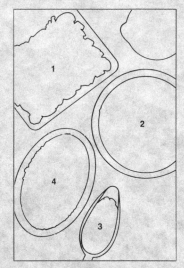

CHOPPED BEEF CASSEROLE

A colorful full meal in a dish. Good way to use leftovers.

Chopped onion	1 cup	250 mL
Chopped celery	⅓ cup	75 mL
All-purpose flour	1 tbsp.	15 mL
Skim milk	1 cup	250 mL
Dry elbow macaroni	1 cup	250 mL
Boiling water	1½ qts.	1.5 L
Condensed tomato soup	10 oz.	284 mL
Cooked carrot coins	2 cups	500 mL
Cooked peas	1 cup	250 mL
Lean chopped cooked roast beef	2 cups	500 mL
Grated low-fat sharp Cheddar cheese (less than 21% MF)	3 tbsp.	50 mL

Spray frying pan with no-stick cooking spray. Add onion and celery. Sauté until soft.

Mix in flour. Stir in milk until it boils and thickens. Remove from heat.

Cook macaroni in boiling water in large uncovered saucepan for 5 to 7 minutes until tender but firm. Drain.

Stir next 4 ingredients together in large bowl. Add onion mixture and macaroni. Mix. Turn into 2 quart (2 L) casserole. Bake, uncovered, in 350° (175°C) oven for about 30 minutes until hot.

Sprinkle with cheese. Bake about 5 minutes more until cheese melts. Makes 6½ cups (1.5 L).

NUTRITION GUIDE	1 cup (225 mL) contains:	
	Energy	258 Calories (1081 kJ)
	Cholesterol	33 mg
	Sodium	434 mg
	Fat	4.4 g

PIZZA

A magic crust topped with hamburger and cheese.

PIZZA CRUST

All-purpose flour	1$\frac{1}{2}$ cups	350 mL
Baking powder	2 tsp.	10 mL
Fast rising yeast	2 tsp.	10 mL
Cooking oil	2 tbsp.	30 mL
Warm water	$\frac{2}{3}$ cup	150 mL

TOPPING

Lean ground beef	$\frac{1}{2}$ lb.	250 g
Tomato paste	$\frac{1}{2}$ cup	125 mL
Water	$\frac{1}{3}$ cup	75 mL
Onion powder	$\frac{1}{4}$ tsp.	1 mL
Garlic powder	$\frac{1}{8}$ tsp.	0.5 mL
Oregano	$\frac{1}{4}$ tsp.	1 mL
Granulated sugar	1 tsp.	5 mL
Basil	$\frac{1}{8}$ tsp.	0.5 mL
Salt	$\frac{1}{2}$ tsp.	2 mL
Pepper	$\frac{1}{8}$ tsp.	0.5 mL
Grated part-skim mozzarella cheese (35% less fat)	1 cup	250 mL
Sliced fresh mushrooms	1 cup	250 mL
Green pepper, in short slivers	1	1
Red pepper, in short slivers	1	1
Grated part-skim mozzarella cheese (35% less fat)	1 cup	250 mL

Pizza Crust: Stir flour, baking powder and yeast together in bowl.

Add cooking oil and water. Mix. Knead on lightly floured surface 25 to 30 times until smooth. Spray 12 inch (30 cm) pizza pan with no-stick cooking spray. Roll and stretch dough to fit pan.

Topping: Spray frying pan with no-stick cooking spray. Add ground beef. Scramble-fry until no pink remains.

Add next 9 ingredients. Stir. Spread over crust.

(continued on next page)

Sprinkle with first amount of cheese.

Arrange mushrooms, green and red peppers over top.

Sprinkle with remaining cheese. Bake on bottom rack in 425°F (220°C) oven for 12 to 15 minutes. Cut into 8 wedges.

NUTRITION GUIDE	1 wedge contains:	
	Energy	267 Calories (1118 kJ)
	Cholesterol	39 mg
	Sodium	335 mg
	Fat	11 g

BEEF HASH

An easy dish and a good way to use leftover roast beef.

Beef bouillon powder (35% less salt)	4 tsp.	20 mL
Finely chopped onion	1 cup	250 mL
Grated raw potato	2½ cups	575 mL
All-purpose flour	2 tbsp.	30 mL
Pepper	½ tsp.	2 mL
Finely chopped lean cooked roast beef	2 cups	500 mL
Water	2 cups	500 mL

Salt to taste

Combine bouillon powder, onion, potato and flour in bowl. Mix. Add pepper, beef and water. Stir. Turn into 2 quart (2 L) casserole. Bake, uncovered, in 350°F (175°C) oven for 1 hour or more until cooked.

Salt to taste. Makes 4½ cups (1 L).

NUTRITION GUIDE	1 cup (225 mL) contains:	
	Energy	210 Calories (877 kJ)
	Cholesterol	44 mg
	Sodium	305 mg
	Fat	3.9 g

LASAGNE

With a real tomato sauce.

MEAT SAUCE

Lean ground beef	1 lb.	454 g
Chopped onion	1 cup	250 mL
Tomato paste	2 × 5½ oz.	2 × 156 mL
Water	1¾ cups	400 mL
White vinegar	1½ tbsp.	25 mL
Chili powder	2 tsp.	10 mL
Oregano	1 tsp.	5 mL
Salt	1 tsp.	5 mL
Garlic powder	¼ tsp.	1 mL
Pepper	¼ tsp.	1 mL
Liquid sweetener	¾ tsp.	4 mL

CHEESE FILLING

Low-fat cottage cheese (less than 1% MF)	2 cups	500 mL
Grated Parmesan cheese	⅓ cup	75 mL
All-purpose flour	2 tbsp.	30 mL
Dried chives	2 tsp.	10 mL
Salt	½ tsp.	2 mL
Pepper	⅛ tsp.	0.5 mL
Skim milk	½ cup	125 mL
Lasagne noodles	9	9
Boiling water	3 qts.	3 L
Grated part-skim mozzarella cheese (35% less fat)	1½ cups	350 mL

Meat Sauce: Spray frying pan with no-stick cooking spray. Add ground beef and onion. Sauté until no pink remains in meat and onion is soft. Transfer to large pot.

Add next 9 ingredients. Heat, stirring occasionally until it boils. Boil slowly for 30 minutes. Add a bit more water if tomato flavor is too strong.

Cheese Filling: Stir first 7 ingredients together in bowl in order given. Set aside.

(continued on next page)

Cook noodles in boiling water in large uncovered pot 14 to 16 minutes until tender but firm. Drain.

To assemble, spray 9 × 13 (22 × 33 cm) pan with no-stick cooking spray and layer as follows:

1. Layer of 3 noodles
2. ½ meat sauce
3. Layer of 3 noodles
4. Cheese filling
5. Layer of 3 noodles
6. ½ of meat sauce
7. Mozzarella cheese

Bake, uncovered, in 350°F (175°C) oven for 45 to 55 minutes until browned. Lay foil over top if cheese browns too soon. Cut into 12 pieces.

NUTRITION GUIDE	1 piece contains:	
	Energy	230 Calories (962 kJ)
	Cholesterol	31 mg
	Sodium	656 mg
	Fat	7 g

A hypnotist used public tranceport to get around.

MEATBALL STEW

Different to have ground beef in a stew. Tasty.

MEATBALLS

Frozen egg product, thawed (low-fat and cholesterol-free)	¼ cup	60 mL
Regular or quick rolled oats (not instant)	½ cup	125 mL
Water	⅓ cup	75 mL
Pepper	¼ tsp.	1 mL
Lean ground beef	¾ lb.	335 g

VEGETABLES

Bite size carrot pieces	2 cups	500 mL
Bite size potato pieces	2 cups	500 mL
Sliced celery	1 cup	250 mL
Sliced onion	1 cup	250 mL
Frozen cut green beans	1 cup	250 mL
Canned tomatoes	19 oz.	540 mL
Beef bouillon powder (35 % less salt)	4 tsp.	20 mL

Meatballs: Place egg product in bowl. Stir in rolled oats, water and pepper.

Add ground beef. Mix. Shape into 24 balls. Arrange on baking sheet. Bake in 425°F (220°C) oven for about 10 minutes to brown.

Vegetables: Combine all 7 ingredients in small roaster. Stir. Cover. Bake in 350°F (175°C) oven for 30 minutes. Add meatballs. Bake about 30 minutes more until carrots are cooked. Makes 6 servings.

NUTRITION GUIDE	1 serving contains:	
	Energy	208 Calories (869 kJ)
	Cholesterol	22 mg
	Sodium	439 mg
	Fat	4.7 g

Simply put all in a roaster and bake. Deep brown tender chunks of meat.

Beef stew meat, trimmed of fat	2 lbs.	900 g
Tomato paste	5½ oz.	156 mL
Water	1 cup	250 mL
Chopped onion	1 cup	250 mL
White vinegar	2 tbsp.	30 mL
Brown sugar	2 tbsp.	30 mL
Light soy sauce (40% less salt)	2 tbsp.	30 mL
Ground ginger	½ tsp.	2 mL
Dry mustard	1 tsp.	5 mL
Beef bouillon powder (35% less salt)	1 tsp.	5 mL
Pepper	¼ tsp.	1 mL

Arrange stew meat in small roaster.

Stir remaining ingredients together in small bowl. Mix. Pour over meat. Cover. Bake in 325°F (160°C) oven for 2½ to 3 hours until very tender. Makes 8 servings.

N U T R I T I O N G U I D E	1 serving contains:	
	Energy	148 Calories (621 kJ)
	Cholesterol	44 mg
	Sodium	244 mg
	Fat	3.7 g

Variation: Short ribs, about 4 lbs. (1.8 kg) may be used instead of stew meat. Fat content will be much higher.

Paré Pointer

Is a fjord a Norwegian car?

CHILI CON CARNE

This oven chili may also be simmered on top of the stove. Extra chili powder may be added if desired.

Lean ground beef	2 lbs.	900 g
All-purpose flour	2 tbsp.	30 mL
Water	2 cups	500 mL
Tomato paste	5½ oz.	156 mL
Chopped onion	3 cups	700 mL
Kidney beans with juice	2 × 14 oz.	2 × 398 mL
Chili powder	1 tbsp.	15 mL
Celery flakes	1 tsp.	5 mL
Cumin	1 tsp.	5 mL
Pepper	¼ tsp.	1 mL
Garlic powder	¼ tsp.	1 mL
Liquid sweetener	1 tsp.	5 mL

Spray frying pan with no-stick cooking spray. Add ground beef. Scramble-fry until browned.

Mix in flour. Add water and tomato paste. Stir until it boils and thickens.

Add remaining ingredients. Stir. Turn into 3 quart (3 L) casserole. Cover. Bake in 350°F (175°C) oven for about 1 hour until flavors are blended. Makes 9¼ cups (2.1 L).

N U T R I T I O N
G U I D E

1 cup (225 mL) contains:

Energy	271 Calories (1133 kJ)
Cholesterol	50 mg
Sodium	386 mg
Fat	8.7 g

Slices of this are very attractive. Ask your meat cutter to slice meat thin enough to roll.

Boiling water	**¼ cup**	**60 mL**
Instant rice, uncooked	**¼ cup**	**60 mL**
Dry bread crumbs	**¾ cup**	**175 mL**
Finely chopped onion	**2 tbsp.**	**30 mL**
Poultry seasoning	**½ tsp.**	**2 mL**
Parsley flakes	**½ tsp.**	**2 mL**
Salt	**½ tsp.**	**2 mL**
Water	**2 tbsp.**	**30 mL**
Lean round steak, thin enough to roll	**2 lbs.**	**900 g**
Canned tomatoes, mashed	**19 oz.**	**540 mL**
Granulated sugar	**½ tsp.**	**2 mL**

Pour boiling water over rice in bowl. Cover. Let stand 5 minutes.

Add next 6 ingredients. Stir.

Lay meat on working surface. Divide rice mixture over meat. Roll up as for jelly roll. Tie with string. Arrange in 3 quart (3 L) casserole.

Stir tomatoes and sugar together and pour over top. Cover. Bake in 350°F (175°C) oven for 1½ to 2 hours until beef is tender. Makes 8 servings.

NUTRITION GUIDE	1 serving contains:	
	Energy	195 Calories (814 kJ)
	Cholesterol	52 mg
	Sodium	390 mg
	Fat	4.8 g

Why don't crabapples taste like seafood?

OVEN BEEF STEW

A good, convenient meaty stew.

Lean beef stewing meat or round steak, cut bite size	1 lb.	454 g
Large onion, cut up	1	1
Medium potatoes, peeled and cut bite size	2	2
Yellow turnip cubes	1 cup	250 mL
Thickly sliced celery	1/2 cup	125 mL
Medium carrots, cut bite size	3	3
Tomato paste	5½ oz.	156 mL
Beef bouillon powder (35% less salt)	4 tsp.	20 mL
Pepper	¼ tsp.	1 mL
Water	1½ cups	375 mL
White vinegar	2 tbsp.	30 mL
Liquid sweetener	¾ tsp.	4 mL

Combine first 6 ingredients in small roaster.

Mix remaining ingredients together in bowl. Pour over top. Cover. Bake in 300°F (150°C) oven for 3 to 4 hours until meat is tender. Makes 4 servings.

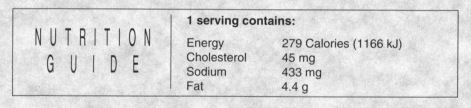

NUTRITION GUIDE	**1 serving contains:**	
	Energy	279 Calories (1166 kJ)
	Cholesterol	45 mg
	Sodium	433 mg
	Fat	4.4 g

An autobiography is really a life history of a car.

Mashed potatoes would add the finishing touch or bake some along side of roaster.

Lean beef pot roast, boneless	4 lbs.	1.8 kg
White wine (or alcohol-free wine)	½ cup	125 mL
Water	½ cup	125 mL
Peppercorns	½ tsp.	2 mL
Bay leaves	2	2
Whole cloves	2	2
Garlic clove, minced	1	1
Salt	1 tsp.	5 mL
Sliced onion	1½ cups	375 mL
Sliced carrots	2 cups	500 mL
Low-fat sour cream (7% MF)	½ cup	125 mL
All-purpose flour	3 tbsp.	50 mL
Boiling water as needed		

Place meat in small roaster. Add next 7 ingredients. Cover. Bake in 325°F (160°C) oven for 1½ hours.

Add onion and carrot. Continue to bake for 1 hour or until meat and vegetables are tender.

Remove vegetables with slotted spoon to bowl. Remove meat to plate. Mix sour cream and flour together. Stir into juice in pan. Heat and stir until it boils and thickens. Turn into measuring cup. Stir in boiling water to make 2 cups (450 mL). Makes 8 servings.

NUTRITION GUIDE	1 serving contains:	
	Energy	315 Calories (1320 kJ)
	Cholesterol	108 mg
	Sodium	443 mg
	Fat	9.7 g

BEEFY CHEESE STEAK

Tender meat in creamy gravy.

Lean round steak, cut in 4 pieces	**1 lb.**	**454 g**
Water	**²/₃ cup**	**150 mL**
Chopped onion	**³/₄ cup**	**175 mL**
Chopped celery	**¹/₂ cup**	**125 mL**
Grated low-fat sharp Cheddar cheese	**¹/₂ cup**	**125 mL**
(less than 21% MF)		
Condensed cream of mushroom soup	**10 oz.**	**284 mL**
Medium potatoes, peeled and sliced	**4**	**4**
Salt and pepper to taste		

Spray frying pan with no-stick cooking spray. Add steak. Brown both sides. Turn into small roaster.

Add water to frying pan. Loosen any brown bits. Pour over meat.

Mix onion, celery, cheese and soup in bowl. Set aside.

Layer potato over meat. Top with soup mixture. Cover. Bake in 350°F (175°C) oven for 1¹/₂ to 2 hours until meat is very tender.

Add salt and pepper to taste. Makes 4 servings.

NUTRITION GUIDE	**1 serving contains:**	
	Energy	414 Calories (1730 kJ)
	Cholesterol	63 mg
	Sodium	764 mg
	Fat	13.2 g

By the time you learn to make the most of life, most of it's gone!

Creamy gravy with yogurt rather than sour cream.

Lean beef sirloin or round steak	**1 lb.**	**454 g**
All-purpose flour	**$\frac{1}{3}$ cup**	**75 mL**
Beef bouillon powder (35% less salt)	**4 tsp.**	**20 mL**
Garlic powder	**$\frac{1}{4}$ tsp.**	**1 mL**
Water	**$1\frac{1}{2}$ cups**	**350 mL**
Low-fat plain yogurt (less than 1% MF)	**1 cup**	**250 mL**
Sliced onion	**1 cup**	**250 mL**
Sliced fresh mushrooms	**1 cup**	**250 mL**
Sherry (or alcohol-free sherry)	**2 tbsp.**	**30 mL**

Spray frying pan with no-stick cooking spray. Cut beef into 4 serving pieces. Brown both sides. Arrange in 2 quart (2 L) casserole.

Combine flour, bouillon powder and garlic powder in saucepan. Mix. Stir in part of the water until no lumps remain. Add rest of water and yogurt. Heat and stir until it boils and thickens.

Add onion, mushrooms and sherry. Stir. Pour over meat. Cover. Bake in 325°F (160°C) oven for 2 hours until meat is tender. Makes 4 servings.

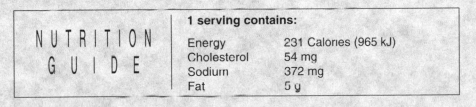

NUTRITION GUIDE

1 serving contains:

Energy	231 Calories (965 kJ)
Cholesterol	54 mg
Sodium	372 mg
Fat	5 g

Paré Pointer

History is a record of events that never should have happened.

CHUNKY CHILI

A different variety. Brown meat, combine with other ingredients and the oven does the rest.

Lean boneless beef, cut in bite size cubes	1½ lbs	680 g
Diced fresh tomatoes (see Note)	2½ cups	575 mL
Canned kidney beans, with juice	14 oz.	398 mL
Chopped onion	1½ cups	375 mL
Chili powder	1 tbsp.	15 mL
Garlic powder	¼ tsp.	1 mL
Pepper	¼ tsp.	1 mL
Oregano	¼ tsp.	1 mL
Granulated sugar	1 tsp.	5 mL

Brown meat under broiler. Drain any juice into small roaster. Turn and brown other side. Transfer meat to roaster.

Mix all remaining ingredients in bowl. Pour over meat. Stir. Cover. Bake in 325°F (160°C) oven for 2 to 2½ hours until meat is very tender. Makes 6 servings.

Pictured on page 53.

NUTRITION GUIDE	1 serving contains:	
	Energy	203 Calories (851 kJ)
	Cholesterol	44 mg
	Sodium	304 mg
	Fat	4 g

Note: One 14 oz. (398 mL) can of tomatoes can be substituted for fresh tomatoes, but sodium content will be higher.

Paré Pointer

The reason there are so many fat dentists is that almost everything they touch is filling.

Similar to a mild chili. Dark reddish color. Add a salad and a dinner roll for a complete meal.

Round steak, fat removed, cut bite size	**1 lb.**	**454 g**
Chopped onion	**1 cup**	**250 mL**
Canned tomatoes, mashed	**19 oz.**	**540 mL**
Instant rice, uncooked	**1 cup**	**250 mL**
Canned kidney beans, with juice	**14 oz.**	**398 mL**
Condensed beef consommé	**10 oz.**	**284 mL**
Chili powder	**1 tsp.**	**5 mL**
Granulated sugar	**½ tsp.**	**2 mL**
Salt	**½ tsp.**	**2 mL**
Pepper	**¼ tsp.**	**1 mL**
Oregano	**¼ tsp.**	**1 mL**

Spray frying pan with no-stick cooking spray. Brown steak and onion. Turn into large bowl.

Stir tomatoes into frying pan to loosen brown bits. Add to bowl.

Add remaining ingredients. Stir well. Turn into 2 quart (2 L) casserole. Cover. Bake in 350°F (175°C) oven for 1½ to 2 hours until meat is tender. Makes 6⅔ cups (1.5 L).

Pictured on page 89.

N U T R I T I O N G U I D E	1 cup (225 mL) contains:	
	Energy	222 Calories (929 kJ)
	Cholesterol	32 mg
	Sodium	819 mg
	Fat	3 g

A man wears trousers, a dog pants.

STEAK MEAL IN A DISH

No pre-browning of meat. Similar to stew.

Boneless sirloin steak, fat removed, cut in slivers	1 lb.	454 g
Thinly sliced onion	1 cup	250 mL
Medium potatoes, peeled and cubed, about 1¼ lbs. (570 g)	4	4
Medium carrots, sliced, about ¾ lb. (340 g)	5	5
Condensed tomato soup	10 oz.	284 mL
Water	1 cup	250 mL
Worcestershire sauce	2 tsp.	10 mL
Salt	1 tsp.	5 mL

Layer steak, onion, potato and carrot in 3 quart (3 L) casserole.

Mix soup, water, Worcestershire sauce and salt in bowl. Pour over top. Cover. Bake in 350°F (175°C) oven for 2 hours or until vegetables are tender. Makes 7⅓ cups (1.65 L).

NUTRITION GUIDE	1 cup (225 mL) contains:	
	Energy	212 Calories (885 kJ)
	Cholesterol	29 mg
	Sodium	735 mg
	Fat	3.1 g

1. Whole Wheat Biscuits page 101
2. Cauliflower-Broccoli Casserole page 148
3. Quick Tamale Casserole page 15
4. Pineapple Ham Pizza page 114
5. Chunky Chili page 50

Prepare rice and chicken ahead to save time.

Chopped fresh mushrooms	2 cups	500 mL
Sesame seeds	2 tbsp.	30 mL
All-purpose flour	3 tbsp.	50 mL
Salt	½ tsp.	2 mL
Skim milk	2 cups	500 mL
Cooked rice	2 cups	500 mL
Chopped cooked chicken breast, skin and fat removed	2 cups	500 mL
Paprika	½ tsp.	2 mL
White wine (or alcohol-free white wine)	¼ cup	60 mL
Hard margarine	1 tbsp.	15 mL
Dry bread crumbs	⅓ cup	75 mL

Spray frying pan with no-stick cooking spray. Add mushrooms and sesame seeds. Sauté until mushrooms are soft.

Mix in flour and salt. Stir in milk until it boils and thickens.

Add rice, chicken, paprika and wine. Stir. Pour into 1½ quart (1.5 L) casserole.

Melt margarine in small saucepan. Stir in bread crumbs. Spread over all. Bake, uncovered, in 350°F (175°C) oven for about 30 to 35 minutes until heated through. Makes 4½ cups (1.1 L).

NUTRITION GUIDE	1 cup (225 mL) contains:	
	Energy	505 Calories (2111 kJ)
	Cholesterol	58 mg
	Sodium	504 mg
	Fat	8.6 g

Paré Pointer

A sleeping child could be a kidnapper.

CHICKEN ZUCCHINI DISH

Serve to your favorite people. Excellent choice.

Dry fettuccine, broken in quarters	4 oz.	125 g
Boiling water	2 qts.	2 L
Boneless chicken breasts, skin and fat removed	1 lb.	454 g
Boiling water to cover		
Chopped onion	⅔ cup	150 mL
Medium zucchini with peel, cut bite size	1	1
Condensed cream of mushroom soup	10 oz.	284 mL
Skim milk	½ cup	125 mL
Grated part-skim mozzarella cheese (35% less fat)	1 cup	250 mL
Garlic powder	¼ tsp.	1 mL
Imitation bacon bits	1 tbsp.	15 mL
Paprika, sprinkle		

Cook fettuccine in first amount of boiling water in large uncovered saucepan about 5 to 7 minutes until tender but firm. Drain.

Cook chicken in second amount of boiling water until tender. Drain. Chop.

Spray frying pan with no-stick cooking spray. Add onion. Sauté until almost soft before adding zucchini. Cover and sauté, stirring often, until zucchini is cooked.

Stir next 5 ingredients together in large bowl until mixed. Add fettuccine, chicken and onion mixture. Stir. Turn into 2 quart (2 L) casserole.

Sprinkle with paprika. Bake, uncovered, in 350°F (175°C) oven for 35 minutes until hot. Makes 6 servings.

NUTRITION GUIDE

1 serving contains:	
Energy	297 Calories (1244 kJ)
Cholesterol	60 mg
Sodium	593 mg
Fat	9.4 g

Variation: Omit paprika. Sprinkle with 1 to 2 tbsp. (15 to 30 mL) grated Parmesan cheese.

One of the best choices you can make. Very good.

Sliced fresh mushrooms	2 cups	500 mL
Dry linguini, broken (or other pasta)	1/2 lb.	250 g
Boiling water	3 qts.	3 L
Coarsely chopped cooked chicken, skin and fat removed	2 cups	500 mL
Minced onion	2 tbsp.	30 mL
Sliced or chopped pimiento-stuffed green olives	1/3 cup	75 mL

SAUCE

All-purpose flour	1/4 cup	60 mL
Salt	3/4 tsp.	4 mL
Pepper	1/4 tsp.	1 mL
Paprika	1/4 tsp.	1 mL
Skim milk	3 cups	750 mL
Grated low-fat medium or sharp Cheddar cheese (less than 21% MF)	1 cup	250 mL
Sherry (or alcohol-free sherry), optional	1 1/2 tbsp.	20 mL

TOPPING

Hard margarine	1 tbsp.	15 mL
Dry bread crumbs	1/3 cup	75 mL

Cook mushrooms and linguini in boiling water in large uncovered pot for 11 to 13 minutes until linguini is tender but firm. Drain.

Add chicken, onion and olives. Stir.

Sauce: Stir flour, salt, pepper and paprika in saucepan. Mix in enough milk to make smooth. Stir in rest of milk and cheese. Add sherry, if desired. Heat and stir until it boils and thickens. Pour over pasta mixture. Stir. Transfer to 3 quart (3 L) casserole.

Topping: Stir margarine and bread crumbs together. Sprinkle over top. Bake, uncovered, in 350°F (175°C) oven for about 30 minutes. Makes 7 cups (1.58 L).

NUTRITION GUIDE	1 cup (225 mL) contains:	
	Energy	360 Calories (1504 kJ)
	Cholesterol	44 mg
	Sodium	708 mg
	Fat	10 g

SPEEDY CHICKEN

A snap to make.

Boneless chicken breasts, skin and fat removed	1½ lbs.	680 g
Ketchup, see page 99	⅓ cup	75 mL
Water	2½ tbsp.	40 mL
Beef bouillon powder (35% less salt)	2 tsp.	10 mL
Onion flakes	2 tsp.	10 mL
Liquid sweetener	½ tsp.	2 mL

Lay chicken in 3 quart (3 L) casserole in single layer.

Stir next 5 ingredients together in bowl. Spoon evenly over chicken pieces. Cover. Bake in 350°F (175°C) oven for 1 to 1½ hours until very tender. Makes 6 servings.

1 serving contains:	
Energy	158 Calories (660 kJ)
Cholesterol	70 mg
Sodium	247 mg
Fat	3 g

HOT CHICKEN SALAD

Enjoy a change. A mild salad tartness. Serve with hot biscuits and plump red tomatoes.

Dry vermicelli (or other thin noodle)	½ lb.	250 g
Boiling water	3 qts.	3 L
Chopped cooked chicken breasts, skin and fat removed	2 cups	500 mL
Thinly sliced celery	1½ cups	375 mL
Sesame seeds, browned in 350°F (175°C) oven, about 5 minutes	1 tbsp.	15 mL
Minced onion	2 tbsp.	30 mL
Chopped pimiento	2 tbsp.	30 mL
Salad dressing, page 98	½ cup	125 mL
Lemon juice, fresh or bottled	1 tbsp.	15 mL
Salt	½ tsp.	2 mL
Grated low-fat sharp Cheddar cheese (less than 21% MF)	2 tbsp.	30 mL
Paprika, sprinkle		

(continued on next page)

Cook vermicelli in boiling water in large uncovered pot for about 4 to 6 minutes until tender but firm. Drain.

In large bowl combine next 8 ingredients. Add vermicelli. Stir well. Turn into 2 quart (2 L) casserole. Bake, uncovered, in 350°F (175°C) oven for 25 minutes until hot.

Sprinkle with cheese then paprika. Continue to bake for about 5 minutes until cheese is melted. Makes 6 servings.

NUTRITION GUIDE	1 serving contains:	
	Energy	332 Calories (1391 kJ)
	Cholesterol	44 mg
	Sodium	432 mg
	Fat	7.6 g

SMOKEY CHICKEN

Try this for campfire flavor.

Boneless chicken breasts, skin and fat removed	2 lbs.	900 g
Condensed cream of mushroom soup	10 oz.	284 mL
Low-fat sour cream (7% MF)	1 cup	250 mL
Liquid smoke	¼ tsp.	1 mL

Spray frying pan with no-stick cooking spray. Brown chicken. Arrange in 3 quart (3 L) casserole.

Mix soup, sour cream and liquid smoke. Pour over chicken. Cover. Bake in 350°F (175°C) oven for about 1 to 1½ hours until tender. Push chicken to the side. Stir sauce to smooth. Makes 8 servings.

NUTRITION GUIDE	1 serving contains:	
	Energy	201 Calories (843 kJ)
	Cholesterol	76 mg
	Sodium	379 mg
	Fat	7.9 g

CHICKEN TETRAZZINI

This is very good even though it doesn't contain the thick cream and rich cheese it usually calls for.

Chicken breasts, halved	1½ lbs.	680 g
Boiling water	2 cups	500 mL
Dry spaghetti, broken	½ lb.	250 g
Boiling water	3 qts.	3 L
Sliced fresh mushrooms	2 cups	500 mL
Red pepper strips	½ cup	125 mL
Sliced green onions	⅓ cup	75 mL
Water	¼ cup	60 mL
All-purpose flour	2 tbsp.	30 mL
Chicken bouillon powder (35% less salt)	2 tsp.	10 mL
Reserved broth	¾ cup	175 mL
Evaporated skim milk	½ cup	125 mL
Sherry (or alcohol-free sherry)	2 tbsp.	30 mL
Grated Parmesan cheese	⅓ cup	75 mL
Salt	½ tsp.	2 mL
Pepper	⅛ tsp.	0.5 mL
Grated low-fat sharp Cheddar cheese (less than 21% MF)	1 cup	250 mL

Cook chicken in first amount of boiling water for about 30 minutes until tender. Drain. Reserve broth. Discard skin and bone. Cut chicken into cubes.

Cook spaghetti in second amount of water in large uncovered saucepan for 11 to 13 minutes until tender but firm. Drain. Add chicken.

Spray frying pan with no-stick cooking spray. Add mushrooms, red pepper and green onion. Sauté until soft.

Mix third amount of water with flour and bouillon powder until no lumps remain. Stir in reserved broth. Pour over mushroom mixture, stirring until it boils and thickens.

(continued on next page)

Add next 5 ingredients. Stir. Add to spaghetti. Stir. Turn into 3 quart (3 L) casserole. Bake in 350°F (175°C) oven for 30 minutes.

Sprinkle with cheese. Bake, uncovered, for about 5 minutes to melt cheese. Makes 7 cups (1.58 L).

N U T R I T I O N G U I D E	1 cup (225 mL) contains:	
	Energy	324 Calories (1354 kJ)
	Cholesterol	57 mg
	Sodium	531 mg
	Fat	7.3 g

CHICKEN RICE BAKE

Colorful with bits of pimiento and parsley showing.

Boneless chicken breasts, skin and fat removed	2 lbs.	900 g
Paprika	½ tsp.	2 mL
Celery salt	½ tsp.	2 mL
Garlic powder	½ tsp.	2 mL
Boiling water	2 cups	500 mL
Chicken bouillon powder (35% less salt)	1 tbsp.	15 mL
Long grain rice, uncooked	1 cup	250 mL
Chopped pimiento	2 tbsp.	30 mL
Parsley flakes	½ tsp.	2 mL

Spray frying pan with no-slick cooking spray. Brown chicken on each side, sprinkling with ½ mixture of paprika, celery salt and garlic powder. Turn and sprinkle with second ½ of mixture.

Pour water into 3 quart (3 L) casserole. Stir in bouillon powder. Add rice, pimiento and parsley. Stir. Lay chicken on top. Cover. Bake in 350°F (175°C) oven for about 1 hour until rice is cooked, water is absorbed and chicken is tender. Makes 8 servings.

Pictured on page 107.

N U T R I T I O N G U I D E	1 serving contains:	
	Energy	212 Calories (888 kJ)
	Cholesterol	70 mg
	Sodium	214 mg
	Fat	3.1 g

CHICKEN ASPARAGUS BAKE

A great combination. The asparagus is hidden beneath the chicken.
A cheesy topping covers it all.

Boneless chicken breasts, skin and fat removed	2 lbs.	900 g
Water	2¹/₂ cups	525 mL
Frozen asparagus	2 × 10 oz.	2 × 284 g
Boiling water		
SAUCE		
All-purpose flour	¹/₂ cup	125 mL
Reserved chicken broth	2 cups	500 mL
Salad dressing, page 98	¹/₂ cup	125 mL
Lemon juice, fresh or bottled	2 tsp.	10 mL
Curry powder	¹/₂ tsp.	2 mL
Salt	¹/₄ tsp.	1 mL
Grated low-fat sharp Cheddar cheese (less than 21% MF)	¹/₂ cup	125 mL
Dry bread crumbs	1 tbsp.	15 mL

Cook chicken breasts in first amount of water for about 30 minutes until tender. Drain. Reserve broth. Remove bones. Chop chicken.

Cook asparagus in some boiling water until tender crisp. Drain. Cut into 1 inch (2.5 cm) lengths. Place in 3 quart (3 L) casserole. Cover with chicken.

Sauce: Mix flour with a little reserved broth in saucepan until no lumps remain. Stir in rest of reserved broth, salad dressing, lemon juice, curry powder and salt. Heat and stir until it boils and thickens. Pour evenly over asparagus.

Stir cheese and bread crumbs together. Sprinkle over top. Cover. Bake in 350°C (175°C) oven for about 30 minutes. Makes 8 servings.

NUTRITION GUIDE	1 serving contains:	
	Energy	233 Calories (976 kJ)
	Cholesterol	74 mg
	Sodium	277 mg
	Fat	4.7 g

Serve over rice or noodles. Lots of vegetables in this.

Boneless chicken breasts, skin and fat removed	1½ lbs.	680 g
Water to cover		
Lemon juice, fresh or bottled	2 tbsp.	30 mL
Sliced celery	1 cup	250 mL
Sliced fresh mushrooms	1 cup	250 mL
Green pepper, seeded and chopped	1	1
Fresh bean sprouts, packed	4 cups	1 L
Chopped onion	¾ cup	175 mL
Water chestnuts, drained and chopped	10 oz.	284 mL
All-purpose flour	3 tbsp.	50 mL
Chicken bouillon powder (35% less salt)	1 tbsp.	15 mL
Pepper	⅛ tsp.	0.5 mL
Reserved broth	1½ cups	350 mL
Light soy sauce (40% less salt)	3 tbsp.	50 mL

Combine first 3 ingredients in large saucepan. Cover. Bring to a boil. Simmer 15 minutes.

Add next 6 ingredients. Return to a boil. Cook for about 10 minutes until tender. Drain. Reserve broth. Remove bones. Cut meat into cubes or slices. Turn chicken and vegetables into 2 quart (2 L) casserole.

Stir flour, bouillon powder and pepper in saucepan. Mix in a little of reserved broth until smooth. Stir in rest of reserved broth and soy sauce. Heat and stir until it boils and thickens. Pour over casserole. Stir lightly. Bake, uncovered, in 350°F (175°C) oven for 25 to 30 minutes. Makes 7 cups (1.58 L).

NUTRITION GUIDE	1 cup (225 mL) contains:	
	Energy	181 Calories (757 kJ)
	Cholesterol	60 mg
	Sodium	471 mg
	Fat	2.9 g

CHICKEN SQUARES

Mild flavored and moist. Red and green specks are attractive showing through the top.

Chopped cooked white chicken meat, skin and fat removed	2 cups	500 mL
Cooked rice	1 cup	250 mL
Dry bread crumbs	¾ cup	175 mL
Chopped celery	¼ cup	60 mL
Frozen egg product, thawed (low-fat and cholesterol-free)	¾ cup	175 mL
Egg white (large)	1	1
Condensed cream of mushroom soup	10 oz.	284 mL
Skim milk	½ cup	125 mL
Chopped pimiento	2 tbsp.	30 mL
Salt	¾ tsp.	4 mL
Thyme	¼ tsp.	1 mL

Combine first 4 ingredients in bowl.

Mix remaining ingredients in bowl. Add to chicken mixture. Stir. Turn into 9 x 9 inch (22 x 22 cm) pan sprayed with no-stick cooking spray. Bake, uncovered, in 350°F (175°C) oven for 50 to 60 minutes until set. Cut into 16 squares to serve.

NUTRITION GUIDE	**1 square contains:**	
	Energy	99 Calories (415 kJ)
	Cholesterol	16 mg
	Sodium	362 mg
	Fat	2.6 g

If you could only combine old automobiles with nylons, you would have cars that run.

Garlic is very light. You may want to strengthen it. Colorful.

Boneless chicken breasts, skin and fat removed	2 lbs.	900 g
Chopped onion	1¼ cups	275 mL
Green pepper, seeded and coarsely chopped	1	1
Sliced fresh mushrooms	1 cup	250 mL
Canned tomatoes, broken up	14 oz.	398 mL
Salt	½ tsp.	2 mL
Pepper	⅛ tsp.	0.5 mL
Garlic powder	¼ tsp	1 mL
White wine (or alcohol-free white wine)	3 tbsp.	50 mL

Arrange chicken in 2 quart (2 L) casserole.

Spray frying pan with no-stick cooking spray. Add onion, green pepper and mushrooms. Sauté until soft. Add to chicken.

Place remaining 5 ingredients in frying pan. Stir to loosen any brown bits. Pour over casserole. Cover. Bake in 350°F (175°C) oven for 1½ hours or until chicken is tender. Makes 8 servings.

Pictured on page 71.

NUTRITION GUIDE	1 serving contains:	
	Energy	162 Calories (679 kJ)
	Cholesterol	70 mg
	Sodium	310 mg
	Fat	3.0 g

A one liner is a Mini Ha Ha.

TOMATO CHICKEN

A different variety of ingredients combine to make this unusual casserole. Currants add to the taste.

Boneless chicken breasts, skin and fat removed	1½ lbs.	680 g
Canned tomatoes	14 oz.	398 mL
Slivered green pepper	¼ cup	60 mL
Chopped onion	½ cup	125 mL
Curry powder	1 tsp.	5 mL
Garlic powder	¼ tsp.	1 mL
Thyme	¼ tsp.	1 mL
Currants	¼ cup	60 mL

Spray frying pan with no-stick cooking spray. Add chicken. Brown both sides. Transfer to 2 quart (2 L) casserole.

Stir remaining ingredients together in bowl. Pour over top. Cover. Bake in 350°F (175°C) oven for 1½ hours until tender. Makes 6 servings.

NUTRITION GUIDE	1 serving contains:	
	Energy	177 Calories (741 kJ)
	Cholesterol	70 mg
	Sodium	168 mg
	Fat	3.0 g

WORTHY CHICKEN

A mild mustard-carrot mixture covers this chicken before being topped with crushed cornflakes.

Boneless chicken breasts, halved, skin and fat removed	1½ lbs.	680 g
Salad dressing, page 98	½ cup	125 mL
Chopped onion	½ cup	125 mL
Grated carrot	½ cup	125 mL
Prepared mustard	1 tbsp.	15 mL
Liquid sweetener	½ tsp.	2 mL
Chives	2 tsp.	10 mL
Thyme	¼ tsp.	1 mL
Basil	¼ tsp.	1 mL
Coarsely crushed corn flakes	½ cup	125 mL

(continued on next page)

Lay chicken in pan large enough to hold single layer.

Mix next 8 ingredients in bowl. Spoon over chicken, getting some on each.

Sprinkle corn flake crumbs over top. Bake, uncovered, in 375°F (190°C) oven for 50 to 60 minutes until tender. Makes 6 servings.

NUTRITION GUIDE	1 serving contains:	
	Energy	209 Calories (872 kJ)
	Cholesterol	71 mg
	Sodium	289 mg
	Fat	3.2 g

CURRIED CHICKEN BAKE

Only a hint of curry. More can easily be added. Also a hint of sweetness and mustard.

Boneless chicken breasts, skin and fat removed	1½ lbs.	680 g
Water	⅓ cup	75 mL
Prepared mustard	1 tbsp.	15 mL
Curry powder	¼ tsp.	1 mL
Cornstarch	2 tsp.	10 mL
Liquid sweetener	½ tsp.	2 mL

Arrange chicken pieces on foil lined baking sheet.

Mix next 5 ingredients in saucepan. Heat and stir until it boils and thickens. Remove from heat. Brush over chicken. Bake, uncovered, in 350°F (175°C) oven for 30 minutes. Turn chicken over. Brush tops. Bake about 15 minutes more or until tender. Makes 6 servings.

NUTRITION GUIDE	1 serving contains:	
	Energy	142 Calories (595 kJ)
	Cholesterol	70 mg
	Sodium	95 mg
	Fat	3.1 g

CHICKEN IN SAUCE

Rich looking gravy with mushrooms and onion.

Boneless chicken breasts, skin and fat removed	1½ lbs.	680 g
Sliced fresh mushrooms	1 cup	250 mL
Sliced onion	1 cup	250 mL
Water	½ cup	125 mL
Tomato paste	1½ tbsp.	25 mL
Sherry (or alcohol-free sherry)	2 tbsp.	30 mL
Paprika	½ tsp.	2 mL
Salt	½ tsp.	2 mL
Pepper	¼ tsp.	1 mL

Spray hot frying pan with no-stick cooking spray. Add chicken. Brown both sides. Transfer to 2 quart (2 L) casserole.

Add mushrooms and onion.

Stir next 6 ingredients together in bowl. Pour over top. Cover. Bake in 350°F (175°C) oven for about 1 hour until tender. Makes 6 servings.

NUTRITION GUIDE

1 serving contains:

Energy	158 Calories (662 kJ)
Cholesterol	70 mg
Sodium	288 mg
Fat	2.9 g

CLUB CHICKEN CASSEROLE

A little salad dressing perks up the flavor in this dish.

Chopped, cooked chicken, skin and fat removed	2 cups	500 mL
Cooked rice	1 cup	250 mL
Salad dressing, page 98	¼ cup	60 mL
Condensed cream of chicken soup	10 oz.	284 mL
Lemon juice, fresh or bottled	1 tbsp.	15 mL
Chopped celery	½ cup	125 mL
Chopped onion	3 tbsp.	50 mL
Sliced fresh mushrooms	1 cup	250 mL
Coarsely crushed corn flakes	½ cup	125 mL

(continued on next page)

Combine first 5 ingredients in bowl.

Spray frying pan with no-stick cooking spray. Add celery, onion and mushrooms. Sauté until soft. Add to chicken mixture. Stir. Turn into 1½ quart (1.5 L) casserole.

Sprinkle corn flake crumbs over top. Bake, uncovered, in 350°F (175°C) oven for 30 to 40 minutes. Makes 4 cups (900 mL).

N U T R I T I O N G U I D E	1 cup (225 mL) contains:	
	Energy	358 Calories (1499 kJ)
	Cholesterol	72 mg
	Sodium	868 mg
	Fat	10.2 g

CHICKEN IN WINE

Just like a classic meal. So easy. A good company casserole.

Boneless chicken breasts, skin and fat removed	2 lbs.	900 g
Condensed cream of mushroom soup	10 oz.	284 mL
Fresh button mushrooms	2 cups	500 mL
White wine (or alcohol-free white wine)	½ cup	125 mL
Pepper	⅛ tsp.	0.5 mL
Paprika	¼ tsp.	1 mL

Arrange chicken in 3 quart (3 L) casserole.

Stir remaining ingredients in bowl. Spoon over top. Bake, covered, in 350°F (175°C) oven for about 1 hour or until tender. Makes 8 servings.

Pictured on cover.

N U T R I T I O N G U I D E	1 serving contains:	
	Energy	181 Calories (757 kJ)
	Cholesterol	70 mg
	Sodium	363 mg
	Fat	5.7 g

CHICKEN COLA

Excellent choice. Lots of juice and carrot sticks to spoon over rice or potatoes.

Boneless chicken breasts, skin and fat removed	**1½ lbs.**	**680 g**
Thinly sliced onion	**½ cup**	**125 mL**
Ketchup, page 99	**½ cup**	**125 mL**
Cola beverage	**1 cup**	**250 mL**
Medium carrots, cut in matchsticks	**2**	**2**

Spray hot frying pan with no-stick cooking spray. Add chicken. Brown. Arrange in 2 quart (2 L) casserole.

Combine next 4 ingredients in bowl. Mix. Pour over chicken. Cover. Bake in 350°F (175°C) oven for 1¼ to 1½ hours until tender. Makes 6 servings.

Pictured on page 125.

NUTRITION GUIDE	1 serving contains:	
	Energy	200 Calories (836 kJ)
	Cholesterol	70 mg
	Sodium	227 mg
	Fat	3 g

1. Corny Biscuits page 103
2. Crowd Pleasing Chili page 14
3. Pork Chops Supreme page 127
4. Chicken Cacciatore page 65
5. Green Pepper Steak page 10

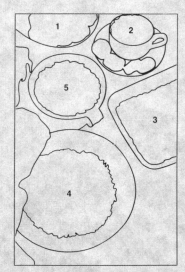

Meat and potatoes in one dish. Each person can add salt to taste.

Chicken breasts, halved, skin and fat removed	2 lbs.	900 g
Water	4 cups	900 mL
Medium potatoes, peeled and halved	3	3
Water		
Chopped onion	½ cup	125 mL
Chopped red or green pepper	½ cup	125 mL
Chicken bouillon powder (35% less salt)	2 tsp.	10 mL
All-purpose flour	2 tbsp.	30 mL
Pepper	⅛ tsp.	0.5 mL
Reserved broth	¾ cup	175 mL
Evaporated skim milk	¼ cup	60 mL
Prepared horseradish	2 tsp.	10 mL

Cook chicken in first amount of water about 30 minutes until tender. Drain, reserving broth. Remove bones. Chop meat. Place in bowl.

Cook potatoes in some water until barely tender. Drain. Cool until you can handle them. Grate coarsely. Add to meat.

Spray frying pan with no-stick cooking spray. Add onion and pepper. Sauté until soft. Add to meat.

In saucepan stir bouillon powder, flour and pepper with enough broth to mix smooth. Add rest of measured broth, milk and horseradish. Heat and stir until it boils and thickens. Add to meat. Stir lightly. Turn into 2 quart (2 L) casserole. Bake, uncovered, in 350°F (175°C) oven for 35 to 45 minutes until hot. Makes 5½ cups (1.24 L).

NUTRITION GUIDE

1 cup (225 mL) contains:

Energy	228 Calories (953 kJ)
Cholesterol	67 mg
Sodium	180 mg
Fat	3 g

CHICKEN EGGS

These eggs are round meatballs served in sauce.

Chicken breasts, halved, skin and fat removed	2¼ lbs.	1 kg
Dry bread crumbs	¾ cup	175 mL
Finely chopped celery	⅓ cup	75 mL
Finely chopped onion	⅓ cup	75 mL
Ground walnuts	⅓ cup	75 mL
Salt	½ tsp.	2 mL
Pepper	⅛ tsp.	0.5 mL
Paprika	¼ tsp.	1 mL
Thyme	⅛ tsp.	0.5 mL
Water	¼ cup	60 mL
SAUCE		
All-purpose flour	2 tbsp.	30 mL
Chicken bouillon powder (35% less salt)	2 tsp.	10 mL
Pepper	⅛ tsp.	0.5 mL
Water	⅔ cup	150 mL
Evaporated skim milk	½ cup	125 mL

Cut meat from bone. Grind meat into bowl.

Add next 9 ingredients. Mix. Shape into 40 balls. Arrange on baking tray. Bake in 350°F (175°C) oven for 25 minutes or until cooked. Turn into 1½ quart (1.5 L) casserole.

Sauce: Stir flour, bouillon powder and pepper together in small saucepan. Add enough water to mix into smooth paste. Stir in rest of water and milk. Heat and stir until it boils and thickens. Pour over chicken eggs. May be held in 200°F (95°C) oven or reheated later. Makes 40 eggs.

Pictured on page 89.

NUTRITION GUIDE

4 eggs contain:

Energy	158 Calories (661 kJ)
Cholesterol	41 mg
Sodium	306 mg
Fat	4.6 g

Good with or without bacon bits. Rice is added before cooking.

Condensed cream of chicken soup	10 oz.	284 mL
Water	1½ cups	375 mL
Juice drained from salmon		
Lemon juice, fresh or bottled	1 tsp.	5 mL
Large hard-boiled eggs, whites only, chopped	2	2
Cut green beans, fresh or frozen	2 cups	500 mL
Canned pink salmon (no added salt), drained, skin and round bones removed	7½ oz.	213 g
Finely chopped onion	⅓ cup	75 mL
Long grain rice, uncooked	1 cup	250 mL
Parsley flakes	1 tsp.	5 mL
Imitation bacon bits (optional)	1 tbsp.	15 mL
Salt to taste (optional)		
Pepper	⅛ tsp.	0.5 mL
Paprika	¼ tsp.	1 mL

Combine all ingredients in order given. Mix. Turn into 3 quart (3 L) casserole. Cover. Bake in 350°F (175°C) oven for 1 to 1¼ hours, stirring at half time to distribute beans, until rice is cooked. Makes 5½ cups (1.24 L).

N U T R I T I O N G U I D E	1 cup (225 mL) contains:	
	Energy	234 Calories (980 kJ)
	Cholesterol	13 mg
	Sodium	530 mg
	Fat	6.5 g

Paré Pointer

Too bad the nuclear scientist swallowed some uranium. Now he has atomic ache.

SALMON RICE BAKE

Contains carrot, onion, broccoli and rice to make a full meal-type casserole.

Water	3 cups	675 mL
Grated carrot, packed	1½ cups	350 mL
Finely chopped onion	1 cup	250 mL
Chicken bouillon powder (35% less salt)	2 tsp.	10 mL
Small broccoli florets	1 cup	250 mL
Instant rice, uncooked	2¼ cups	500 mL
Condensed cream of mushroom soup	10 oz.	284 mL
Canned pink salmon (no added salt), drained, skin and round bones removed	7½ oz.	213 g
Paprika, sprinkle		

Combine water, carrot, onion and bouillon powder in saucepan. Cover and cook until onion is almost tender.

Add broccoli. Cook for 4 minutes more. Do not drain.

Stir in rice. Cover. Let stand 5 minutes.

Add soup. Stir to mix. Break up salmon. Stir in. Turn into 2 quart (2 L) casserole.

Sprinkle with paprika. Cover. Bake in 350°F (175°C) oven for 30 minutes. Makes 6⅓ cups (1.43 L).

NUTRITION GUIDE	1 cup (225 mL) contains:	
	Energy	254 Calories (1065 kJ)
	Cholesterol	8 mg
	Sodium	538 mg
	Fat	6.6 g

Paré Pointer

A sign by a tree and fire hydrant said "Get a lawn, little doggie, get a lawn".

Although this should be served immediately, the topping will stay soft and tasty for a lengthy spell.

All-purpose flour	¹/₂ **cup**	**125 mL**
Paprika	¹/₄ **tsp.**	**1 mL**
Celery salt	¹/₄ **tsp.**	**1 mL**
Salt	¹/₄ **tsp.**	**1 mL**
Skim milk	1¹/₂ **cups**	**350 mL**
Water packed tuna, drained and flaked	6¹/₂ **oz.**	**184 g**
Parsley flakes	¹/₂ **tsp.**	**2 mL**
Egg whites (large), room temperature	**4**	**4**
Baking powder	¹/₂ **tsp.**	**2 mL**

Stir flour, paprika, celery salt and salt together in saucepan. Mix in some of the milk until no lumps remain. Add rest of milk. Heat and stir until it boils and thickens. Remove from heat.

Add tuna and parsley.

Beat egg whites and baking powder in mixing bowl until stiff. Fold into tuna mixture. Pour into 2 quart (2 L) casserole that bottom has been sprayed with no-stick cooking spray. Bake in 350°F (175°C) oven for 30 to 35 minutes until it looks puffy and golden brown. Center will be soft. Makes 4 servings.

N U T R I T I O N G U I D E	**1 serving contains:**	
	Energy	170 Calories (712 kJ)
	Cholesterol	10 mg
	Sodium	528 mg
	Fat	.6 g

At an auction sale you can very easily get something for nodding.

TUNA SHELL CASSEROLE

Stuffed shells over creamed spinach. A tasteful go-together.

Giant pasta shells	**18**	**18**
Boiling water	**3 qts.**	**3 L**
All-purpose flour	**3 tbsp.**	**50 mL**
Salt	**$\frac{1}{4}$ tsp.**	**1 mL**
Pepper	**$\frac{1}{8}$ tsp.**	**0.5 mL**
Nutmeg	**$\frac{1}{8}$ tsp.**	**0.5 mL**
Skim milk	**1 cup**	**250 mL**
Frozen chopped spinach, cooked and drained	**10 oz.**	**284 g**
Part-skim ricotta cheese, broken up	**$\frac{1}{2}$ lb.**	**227 g**
Water packed tuna, drained and flaked	**$6\frac{1}{2}$ oz.**	**184 g**
Paprika, sprinkle		

Cook shells in boiling water in uncovered Dutch oven about 12 to 15 minutes until tender but firm. Drain. Rinse with cold water. Drain well.

Measure next 4 ingredients into saucepan. Whisk in some milk until no lumps remain, then whisk in rest of milk. Heat and stir until it boils and thickens.

Stir in spinach. Turn into 8 x 8 inch (20 x 20 cm) baking dish.

Mash cheese and tuna together. Carefully stuff shells. Arrange over spinach.

Sprinkle with paprika. Cover. Bake in 350°F (175°C) oven for 20 to 30 minutes until heated through. Makes 6 servings.

NUTRITION GUIDE	1 serving contains:	
	Energy	225 Calories (940 kJ)
	Cholesterol	18 mg
	Sodium	334 mg
	Fat	3.8 g

Paré Pointer

Sometimes it doesn't matter who you know but who you yes.

Serve this with noodles for a satisfying meal.

All-purpose flour	**¹/₃ cup**	**75 mL**
Skim milk	**¹/₃ cup**	**75 mL**
Skim milk	**1¹/₂ cups**	**350 mL**
Chives	**2 tsp.**	**10 mL**
Onion flakes	**2 tsp.**	**10 mL**
Salt	**¹/₂ tsp.**	**2 mL**
Pepper	**¹/₄ tsp.**	**1 mL**
Sherry (or alcohol-free sherry)	**¹/₄ cup**	**60 mL**
Frozen peas	**1 cup**	**250 mL**
Cooked shrimp, chopped	**12 oz.**	**340 g**
Grated low-fat sharp Cheddar cheese (less than 21% MF)	**¹/₂ cup**	**125 mL**

Stir flour and first amount of skim milk together in saucepan until no lumps remain.

Add next 5 ingredients. Heat and stir until it comes to a boil and thickens.

Stir in remaining ingredients. Turn into 1 quart (1 L) casserole. Bake, uncovered, in 350°F (175°C) oven for about 45 minutes. Makes 4 servings.

N U T R I T I O N G U I D E	**1 serving contains:**	
	Energy	271 Calories (1132 kJ)
	Cholesterol	174 mg
	Sodium	688 mg
	Fat	5.3 g

When liars die they lie still.

SEAFOOD CASSEROLE

A meal deluxe.

Long grain rice	³/₄ cup	175 mL
Boiling water	1¹/₂ cups	350 mL
Sliced fresh mushrooms	2 cups	500 mL
Diced celery	1 cup	250 mL
Diced green pepper (optional)	¹/₃ cup	75 mL
All-purpose flour	3 tbsp.	50 mL
Salt	¹/₂ tsp.	2 mL
Skim milk	2¹/₂ cups	600 mL
Salad dressing, page 98	¹/₂ cup	125 mL
Cooked peas	1 cup	250 mL
Onion flakes	1 tbsp.	15 mL
Worcestershire sauce	1 tbsp.	15 mL
Curry powder	¹/₂ tsp.	2 mL
Imitation crabmeat, sliced	¹/₄ lb.	120 g
Cooked shrimp	¹/₄ lb.	120 g
TOPPING		
Hard margarine	1 tbsp.	15 mL
Dry bread crumbs	¹/₃ cup	75 mL

Cook rice in boiling water until tender and water is absorbed.

Spray frying pan with no-stick cooking spray. Add mushrooms, celery and green pepper. Sauté until soft.

Mix in flour and salt. Stir in milk until it boils and thickens.

Add next 7 ingredients along with rice. Stir. Turn into 2 quart (2 L) casserole.

Topping: Melt margarine in small saucepan. Stir in bread crumbs. Spread over casserole. Bake, uncovered, in 350°F (175°C) oven for about 45 minutes until very hot. Makes 6¹/₂ cups (1.5 L).

NUTRITION GUIDE	1 cup (225 mL) contains:	
	Energy	246 Calories (1029 kJ)
	Cholesterol	39 mg
	Sodium	663 mg
	Fat	3.2 g

Slightly crunchy, this really stretches a can of tuna.

Condensed cream of mushroom soup	**10 oz.**	**284 mL**
Water	**²/₃ cup**	**150 mL**
Cooked noodles	**1 cup**	**250 mL**
Finely chopped celery	**1 cup**	**250 mL**
Finely chopped onion	**¹/₂ cup**	**125 mL**
Finely chopped green pepper	**¹/₄ cup**	**50 mL**
Chopped water chestnuts, drained	**5 oz.**	**142 mL**
Cracker crumbs (unsalted)	**³/₄ cup**	**175 mL**
Water-packed tuna, drained and flaked	**2 × 6¹/₂ oz.**	**2 × 184 g**
Pepper	**¹/₈ tsp.**	**0.5 mL**
Chow mein noodles	**¹/₄ cup**	**60 mL**

Mix soup and water in medium bowl.

Add next 8 ingredients. Stir. Turn into 1¹/₂ quart (1.5 L) casserole.

Sprinkle with noodles. Bake, uncovered, in 350°F (175°C) oven for about 45 minutes. Makes 5 cups (1.13 L).

Pictured on page 17.

NUTRITION GUIDE	1 cup (225 mL) contains:	
	Energy	287 Calories (1199 kJ)
	Cholesterol	14 mg
	Sodium	941 mg
	Fat	7.6 g

Paré Pointer

People who sculpt, bathe often so they won't be known as dirty chiselers.

FISH PIE

Complete the meal with a green vegetable.

Sole, cod or other white fish fillets	**1 lb.**	**454 g**
Water to cover		
Medium potatoes, peeled and halved	**3**	**3**
Water		
Skim milk	**¼ cup**	**60 mL**
All-purpose flour	**3 tbsp.**	**50 mL**
Skim milk	**⅔ cup**	**150 mL**
Reserved fish stock	**½ cup**	**125 mL**
Parsley flakes	**½ tsp.**	**2 mL**
Grated low-fat sharp Cheddar cheese	**½ cup**	**125 mL**
(21% less MF)		
Onion flakes	**2 tbsp.**	**30 mL**
Paprika, sprinkle		

Cook fish in water for about 5 minutes until it flakes easily. Drain, reserving ½ cup fish stock. Flake fish. Set aside.

Cook potatoes in some water until tender. Drain. Mash.

Add first amount of milk. Mash again.

Mix flour with some of the second amount of milk until no lumps remain. Stir in remaining milk. Heat and stir until it boils and thickens.

Add next 4 ingredients. Add fish. Stir. Turn into 1½ quart (1.5 L) casserole. Cover with potatoes.

Sprinkle with paprika. Bake, uncovered, in 350°F (175°C) oven for about 40 minutes until hot and browned. Makes 4 servings.

NUTRITION GUIDE	1 serving contains:	
	Energy	279 Calories (1167 kJ)
	Cholesterol	59 mg
	Sodium	199 mg
	Fat	4 g

This looks so fancy yet is so easy to make. Not actually a casserole but you serve it from the oven.

Canned pink salmon (no added salt), drained, skin and round bones removed	2 × 7¹/₂ oz.	2 × 213 g
Finely chopped celery	²/₃ cup	150 mL
Salad dressing, page 98	¹/₃ cup	75 mL
Onion powder	¹/₂ tsp.	2 mL
Chives	1¹/₂ tsp.	7 mL

BISCUIT DOUGH

All-purpose flour	2 cups	450 mL
Baking powder	4 tsp.	20 mL
Salt	¹/₄ tsp.	1 mL
Cayenne pepper	¹/₈ tsp.	0.5 mL
Vegetable cooking oil	2 tbsp.	30 mL
Skim milk	⁷/₈ cup	200 mL

Combine first 5 ingredients in bowl. Stir well.

Biscuit Dough: Measure flour, baking powder, salt and cayenne pepper into a separate bowl. Stir.

Add cooking oil and milk. Mix until soft ball forms. Knead on lightly floured surface 6 to 8 times. Roll out to 12 inch (30 cm) square. Spread with salmon mixture. Roll up like jelly roll. Dampen and seal seam. Cut into 12 slices. Arrange cut side down on pan that has been sprayed with no-stick cooking spray. Bake in 400°F (205°C) oven for 20 to 25 minutes until browned. Makes 12 servings.

Pictured on cover.

NUTRITION GUIDE	1 serving contains:	
	Energy	159 Calories (664 kJ)
	Cholesterol	9 mg
	Sodium	136 mg
	Fat	5.2 g

SHRIMP NOODLE CASSEROLE

Also contains kernel corn. Creamy with a browned cheese topping.

Dry fettuccine	8 oz.	250 g
Boiling water	2 qts.	2 L
Frozen kernel corn, cooked	1½ cups	375 mL
Sliced fresh mushrooms	1 cup	250 mL
Frozen cooked shrimp	½ lb.	250 g
SAUCE		
All-purpose flour	3 tbsp.	50 mL
Salt	½ tsp.	2 mL
Pepper	⅛ tsp.	0.5 mL
Powdered skim milk	⅓ cup	75 mL
Skim milk	2 cups	500 mL
Reserved juice from shrimp		
Paprika	¼ tsp.	1 mL
Grated low-fat sharp Cheddar cheese (less than 21% MF)	1½ cups	375 mL

Cook fettuccine in boiling water in large uncovered pot for 5 to 7 minutes until tender but firm. Drain. Turn into 3 quart (3 L) casserole.

Spread corn over noodles followed by mushrooms then shrimp.

Sauce: Measure flour, salt, pepper and powdered milk (which adds extra richness) into saucepan. Add enough milk to mix until no lumps remain. Stir in rest of milk, juice from shrimp and paprika. Heat and stir over medium heat until it boils and thickens.

Stir in 1 cup (250 mL) of the grated cheese. Pour over shrimp. Bake, uncovered, in 350°F (175°C) oven for 30 minutes until heated through. Sprinkle with remaining cheese. Return to oven for about 5 minutes to melt cheese. Makes 7½ cups (1.7 L).

Pictured on page 143.

NUTRITION GUIDE	1 cup (225 mL) contains:	
	Energy	331 Calories (1386 kJ)
	Cholesterol	80 mg
	Sodium	463 mg
	Fat	6.6 g

A tuna-based sauce cooked over broccoli makes for a great meal.

Sliced fresh mushrooms	**2 cups**	**500 mL**
Skim milk	**1¼ cups**	**275 mL**
Salt	**½ tsp.**	**2 mL**
Pepper	**⅛ tsp.**	**0.5 mL**
Garlic powder	**⅛ tsp.**	**0.5 mL**
Sliced green onion	**¼ cup**	**60 mL**
Chopped pimiento	**2 tbsp.**	**30 mL**
Water-packed tuna, drained and flaked	**2 × 6½ oz.**	**2 × 184 g**
All-purpose flour	**¼ cup**	**60 mL**
Skim milk	**¼ cup**	**60 mL**
Broccoli, cut bite size	**1 lb.**	**454 g**
Boiling water		
Grated low-fat sharp Cheddar cheese	**¼ cup**	**60 mL**
(less than 21% MF)		
Dry bread crumbs	**¼ cup**	**60 mL**

Spray frying pan with no-stick cooking spray. Add mushrooms. Sauté until moisture has evaporated.

Add next 7 ingredients. Stir.

Mix flour and second amount of skim milk in small bowl until no lumps remain. Stir into tuna mixture until it boils and thickens. Remove from heat.

Cook broccoli in some boiling water until barely tender. Drain. Scatter over bottom of 3 quart (3 L) casserole. Pour tuna mixture over top.

Sprinkle with cheese, then bread crumbs. Bake, uncovered, in 350°F (175°C) oven for 30 minutes until bubbly hot. Makes 5½ cups (1.25 L).

NUTRITION GUIDE	1 cup (225 mL) contains:	
	Energy	200 Calories (835 kJ)
	Cholesterol	16 mg
	Sodium	611 mg
	Fat	2.2 g

BAKED FILLETS

The red pepper makes this tasty dish quite colorful.

Cod fish fillets	1 lb.	454 g
Light soy sauce (40% less salt)	2 tsp.	10 mL
Lemon juice, fresh or bottled	2 tsp.	10 mL
Garlic powder	$1/8$ tsp.	0.5 mL
Ginger, just a pinch		
Granulated sugar	$3/4$ tsp.	4 mL
Chopped green onion	$1/3$ cup	75 mL
Sliced fresh mushrooms	$1\frac{1}{2}$ cups	375 mL
Small red pepper, seeded and cut in slivers	1	1

Arrange fish fillets in 2 quart (2 L) casserole.

Mix next 5 ingredients. Brush over fish. Reserve rest of marinade.

Sprinkle with onion, mushrooms and red pepper. Cover. Bake in 400°F (205°C) oven for 20 to 30 minutes. Dab with marinade mixture at half time. When fish flakes easily with a fork it is done. Makes 4 servings.

NUTRITION GUIDE	1 serving contains:	
	Energy	114 Calories (478 kJ)
	Cholesterol	49 mg
	Sodium	176 mg
	Fat	1 g

1. Green Pea Bake page 145
2. Tuna Squares page 96
3. Chicken Eggs page 74
4. Meat And Rice Casserole page 51

Add a salad to make this more complete.

Water	2½ cups	575 mL
Chopped onion	⅔ cup	150 mL
Grated carrot	1 cup	250 mL
Chopped fresh mushrooms	½ cup	125 mL
Lemon juice, fresh or bottled	2 tsp.	10 mL
Instant rice, uncooked	1¼ cups	300 mL
Skim milk	⅓ cup	75 mL
All-purpose flour	⅓ cup	75 mL
Chicken bouillon powder (35% less salt)	1 tsp.	5 mL
Cayenne pepper	⅛ tsp.	0.5 mL
Paprika	⅛ tsp.	0.5 mL
Skim milk	1 cup	250 mL
Peas, fresh or frozen, thawed	10 oz.	284 g
Canned pink salmon (no added salt), drained, skin and round bones removed	7½ oz.	213 g

TOPPING

Grated low-fat sharp Cheddar cheese (less than 21% MF)	¼ cup	60 mL
Dry bread crumbs	¼ cup	60 mL

Measure first 5 ingredients into saucepan. Cover. Cook until vegetables are tender. Do not drain.

Add rice. Stir. Let stand 5 minutes.

Whisk first amount of milk with flour, bouillon powder, cayenne pepper and paprika until smooth. Add second amount of milk. Heat and stir until it boils and thickens.

Stir in peas and salmon. Add to rice mixture. Stir. Turn into 2 quart (2 L) casserole. Bake, uncovered, in 350°F (175°C) oven for 25 minutes.

Topping: Stir cheese and bread crumbs together. Sprinkle over casserole. Continue to bake for about 15 minutes more. Makes 7 cups (1.58 L).

NUTRITION GUIDE	1 cup (225 mL) contains:	
	Energy	222 Calories (931 kJ)
	Cholesterol	10 mg
	Sodium	537 mg
	Fat	6.8 g

SHRIMP CREOLE

This is a runny mixture that is served over rice. Excellent. Serve from stove top or from oven.

Chopped onion	**2 cups**	**500 mL**
Chopped celery	**2 cups**	**500 mL**
Boiling water		
Skim milk	**1 cup**	**250 mL**
All-purpose flour	**2 tbsp.**	**30 mL**
Skim milk	**2 tbsp.**	**30 mL**
Condensed tomato soup	**10 oz.**	**284 mL**
Salt	**¼ tsp.**	**1 mL**
Pepper	**⅛ tsp.**	**0.5 mL**
Fresh medium shrimp, cooked	**¾ lb.**	**375 g**

Cook onion and celery in some boiling water until tender. Drain through sieve.

Heat first amount of milk in saucepan until it boils.

Mix flour with second amount of milk until no lumps remain. Stir into boiling milk until it returns to a boil and thickens.

Stir in soup, salt and pepper.

Add shrimp to soup mixture reserving a few for garnish. Turn into 1½ quart (1.5 L) casserole. Cover. May be held in 200°F (95°C) oven for at least 2 hours or may be chilled in refrigerator for next-day use. Heat in 350°F (175°C) oven for 25 to 30 minutes until hot. Garnish with shrimp the last 5 to 10 minutes. Makes 4⅓ cups (1 L).

Pictured on page 35.

N U T R I T I O N G U I D E	½ cup (125 mL) contains:	
	Energy	133 Calories (555 kJ)
	Cholesterol	91 mg
	Sodium	483 mg
	Fat	1.8 g

Variation: Omit fresh shrimp. Use 2 x 4 oz. (2 x 113 g) cans of medium cleaned shrimp. Sodium per serving will increase.

SHRIMP WITH RICE

A meal in one. Good flavor.

Chopped onion	1 cup	250 mL
Chopped fresh mushrooms	1 cup	250 mL
Chopped green pepper	1/3 cup	75 mL
Worcestershire sauce	1 tsp.	5 mL
Chopped celery	1/2 cup	125 mL
Water	2 cups	500 mL
Condensed cream of mushroom soup	10 oz.	284 mL
Reserved juice, plus water if needed	1/2 cup	125 mL
Long grain rice	2/3 cup	150 mL
Boiling water	1 1/3 cups	300 mL
Cooked fresh shrimp	2 cups	500 mL
Corn flake crumbs	3 tbsp.	50 mL

Combine first 6 ingredients in saucepan. Cook until tender. Drain and reserve juice.

Stir in soup and reserved juice.

Cook rice in boiling water for about 15 minutes until tender and water is absorbed. Add to vegetable mixture.

Stir in shrimp. Turn into 2 quart (2 L) casserole.

Sprinkle corn flake crumbs over top. Cook, uncovered, in 350°F (175°C) oven for 20 to 30 minutes until bubbly hot. Makes 5 2/3 cups (1.28 L).

NUTRITION GUIDE	1 cup (225 mL) contains:	
	Energy	212 Calories (888 kJ)
	Cholesterol	92 mg
	Sodium	577 mg
	Fat	5.4 g

SHRIMP IMPERIAL

A special luncheon dish.

Low-fat cottage cheese (less than 1% MF)	½ cup	125 mL
White vinegar	1½ tsp.	7 mL
All-purpose flour	3 tbsp.	50 mL
Dry mustard	⅛ tsp.	0.5 mL
Chicken bouillon powder (35% less salt)	1 tsp.	5 mL
Skim milk	1 cup	250 mL
Canned chicken, broken up	6¼ oz.	184 g
Canned medium shrimp, drained	4 oz.	113 g
Sherry (or alcohol-free sherry)	2 tbsp.	30 mL
Paprika	¼ tsp.	1 mL
TOPPING		
Hard margarine	1 tbsp.	15 mL
Dry bread crumbs	⅓ cup	75 mL

Smooth cottage cheese, vinegar, flour, mustard and bouillon powder in blender.

Heat milk in saucepan until it boils. Stir cottage cheese mixture into boiling milk until it returns to a boil and thickens.

Add next 4 ingredients. Stir. Turn into 1 quart (1 L) casserole.

Topping: Melt margarine in small saucepan. Stir in bread crumbs. Sprinkle over top. Bake, uncovered, in 350°F (175°C) oven for 20 to 25 minutes until bubbly hot. Makes 4 servings.

NUTRITION GUIDE	1 serving contains:	
	Energy	238 Calories (996 kJ)
	Cholesterol	74 mg
	Sodium	602 mg
	Fat	8 g

SHRIMP AND RICE CREOLE

Good tomato flavor with lots of shrimp.

Long grain rice	²/₃ cup	150 mL
Boiling water	1¹/₃ cups	300 mL
Medium shrimp, shelled and deveined	1 lb.	454 g
Boiling water	1¹/₂ cups	375 mL
Chopped onion	¹/₂ cup	125 mL
Chopped green pepper	¹/₄ cup	60 mL
Sliced fresh mushrooms	1 cup	250 mL
Tomato paste	5¹/₂ oz.	156 mL
Water	³/₄ cup	175 mL
Granulated sugar	1 tsp.	5 mL
Salt	¹/₂ tsp.	2 mL
Pepper	¹/₄ tsp.	1 mL
TOPPING		
Hard margarine	1 tbsp.	15 mL
Dry bread crumbs	¹/₃ cup	75 mL

Cook rice in first amount of water about 15 minutes until tender and water is absorbed. Set aside.

Cook shrimp in second amount of water for about 5 minutes until pinkish and curled a bit. Drain. Cut up into bite size pieces. Set aside.

Spray frying pan with no-stick cooking spray. Add onion, green pepper and mushrooms. Sauté until soft.

In medium size bowl mix tomato paste, third amount of water, sugar, salt and pepper. Add prepared rice, shrimp and onion mixture. Stir. Turn into 1¹/₂ quart (1.5 L) casserole.

Topping: Melt margarine in small saucepan. Stir in bread crumbs. Spread over casserole. Bake, uncovered, in 350°F (175°C) oven for 30 minutes. Makes 5 cups (1.13 L).

NUTRITION GUIDE	1 cup (225 mL) contains:	
	Energy	257 Calories (1076 kJ)
	Cholesterol	138 mg
	Sodium	508 mg
	Fat	4.8 g

OVEN FRIED FISH

What a nice change to have this cooked in the oven.

Lemon juice, fresh or bottled	1½ tsp.	7 mL
Low-fat cottage cheese (less than 1% MF)	½ cup	125 mL
Dry onion soup mix	1 tbsp.	15 mL
Fine dry bread crumbs	½ cup	125 mL
Grated Parmesan cheese	1 tbsp.	15 mL
Parsley flakes	½ tsp.	2 mL
Paprika	¼ tsp.	1 mL
Fish fillets, 4 oz. (112 g) size	4	4

Run lemon juice and cottage cheese through blender to smooth. Turn into bowl.

Stir dry soup mixture well, then measure required amount. Stir into cottage cheese mixture.

In another small bowl mix bread crumbs, cheese, parsley and paprika.

Spray baking pan with no-stick cooking spray. Spread fish with cottage cheese mixture then roll in crumb mixture. Arrange on baking pan. Bake in 400°F (205°C) oven about 20 minutes until browned and fish flakes easily with fork. Makes 4 servings.

N U T R I T I O N G U I D E	1 serving contains:	
	Energy	188 Calories (787 kJ)
	Cholesterol	51 mg
	Sodium	659 mg
	Fat	2.3 g

TUNA SQUARES

This could almost pass for chicken.

Large eggs	2	2
Skim milk	1 cup	250 mL
Dry bread crumbs	1 cup	250 mL
Finely chopped onion	⅓ cup	75 mL
Parsley flakes	1 tsp.	5 mL
Lemon juice, fresh or bottled	1 tbsp.	15 mL
Salt	¾ tsp.	4 mL
Pepper	¼ tsp.	1 mL
Thyme, generous measure	¼ tsp.	1 mL
Water-packed tuna, drained and flaked	3 × 6½ oz.	3 × 184 g

(continued on next page)

Beat eggs in medium bowl until frothy.

Add remaining ingredients, stirring after each addition. Turn into 8 x 8 inch (20 x 20 cm) pan that has been sprayed with no-stick cooking spray. Bake in 350°F (175°C) oven for 40 minutes until firm. Cut into 9 squares.

Pictured on page 89.

NUTRITION GUIDE	1 square contains:	
	Energy	160 Calories (671 kJ)
	Cholesterol	59 mg
	Sodium	585 mg
	Fat	2 g

GARLIC TOAST

Tastes like the real thing but with very little fat.

Diet soft margarine	**4 tbsp.**	**60 mL**
Garlic powder	**½ tsp.**	**2 mL**
French loaf slices, 1 inch (2.5 cm) thick	**12**	**12**

Mix margarine with garlic powder in small bowl.

Arrange bread slices on baking sheet. Toast under broiler. Turn slices over. Spread each slice with 1 tsp. (5 mL) margarine mixture. Toast again under broiler. Makes 12 slices.

NUTRITION GUIDE	1 slice contains:	
	Energy	134 Calories (561 kJ)
	Cholesterol	trace
	Sodium	273 mg
	Fat	2.1 g

SEEDY TOAST

Quick and easy.

Diet soft margarine	4 tbsp.	60 mL
Celery seed	1 tsp.	5 mL
Onion powder	¼ tsp.	1 mL
Paprika	¼ tsp.	1 mL
Hot pepper sauce	¼ tsp.	1 mL
French loaf slices, 1 inch (2.5 cm) thick	12	12

Mix first 5 ingredients in bowl.

Arrange bread slices on broiler tray. Broil to toast 1 side. Turn slices over. Spread untoasted side with 1 tsp. (5 mL) margarine mixture. Broil to toast. Serve hot. Makes 12 slices.

NUTRITION GUIDE

1 slice contains:

Energy	135 Calories (563 kJ)
Cholesterol	trace
Sodium	274 mg
Fat	2.2 g

SALAD DRESSING

For the lowest fat content, make your own.

Granulated sugar	¼ cup	60 mL
All-purpose flour	3 tbsp.	50 mL
Dry mustard powder	½ tsp.	2 mL
Salt	½ tsp.	2 mL
Skim milk	1 cup	250 mL
White vinegar	¼ cup	60 mL

Stir first 4 ingredients together well in small saucepan.

Mix in part of the milk until smooth. Whisk in remaining milk and vinegar. Heat and stir until it boils and thickens. Pour into container when cooled a bit. Store in refrigerator. Makes 1¼ cups (275 mL).

NUTRITION GUIDE

1 tbsp. (15 mL) contains:

Energy	19 Calories (80 kJ)
Cholesterol	trace
Sodium	75 mg
Fat	trace

Use as a condiment or in recipes requiring ketchup.

Tomato paste	5$\frac{1}{2}$ oz.	156 mL
Water	$\frac{1}{3}$ cup	75 mL
White vinegar	$\frac{1}{2}$ cup	125 mL
Granulated sugar	$\frac{1}{4}$ cup	60 mL
Onion powder	$\frac{3}{4}$ tsp.	4 mL
Salt	$\frac{3}{4}$ tsp.	4 mL
Ground cloves	$\frac{1}{8}$ tsp.	0.5 mL
Cornstarch	1 tbsp.	15 mL
Water	3 tbsp.	50 mL
Liquid sweetener	1$\frac{1}{2}$ tsp.	7 mL

Place first 7 ingredients in saucepan. Heat and stir on medium-high until it boils.

Mix cornstarch, water and sweetener together in small cup. Stir into boiling liquid until it boils and thickens. Cool. Makes 1$\frac{1}{4}$ cups (300 mL).

NUTRITION GUIDE	1 tbsp. (15 mL) contains:	
	Energy	20 Calories (82 kJ)
	Cholesterol	0 mg
	Sodium	108 mg
	Fat	trace

Serve with meat, especially chicken and turkey.

Cranberries, fresh or frozen	2 cups	450 mL
Water	$\frac{3}{4}$ cup	175 mL
Liquid sweetener	2 tsp.	10 mL

Place cranberries and water in saucepan. Bring to a boil. Boil slowly for about 10 minutes until berries pop their skins.

Stir in sweetener. Cool. Store in refrigerator. Makes 1$\frac{1}{3}$ cups (300 mL).

NUTRITION GUIDE	1 tbsp. (15 mL) contains:	
	Energy	4 Calories (19 kJ)
	Cholesterol	0 mg
	Sodium	trace
	Fat	trace

BANNOCK BISCUITS MODERN

A different biscuit to be sure. Cooked in a modern appliance rather than over a fire.

Whole wheat flour	1½ cups	350 mL
Cornmeal	½ cup	125 mL
Baking powder	1 tbsp.	15 mL
Salt	½ tsp.	2 mL
Skim milk	1½ cups	350 mL
Granulated sugar	2 tbsp.	30 mL

Stir first 4 ingredients together in bowl.

Add milk and sugar. Stir just until mixture is moistened. Mixture should be thick and barely spreadable. Spray frying pan with no-stick cooking spray. Spread about ¼ cup (60 mL) batter in flattish circle. An ice cream scoop is ideal for this. Try 1 first to be sure pan isn't too hot. An electric frying pan would be 325°F (160°C). Cover. Cook for about 9 minutes without turning. Tops will feel dry and firm and bottoms will be browned. Makes 10 large biscuits.

Pictured on page 17.

NUTRITION GUIDE	1 biscuit contains:	
	Energy	108 Calories (451 kJ)
	Cholesterol	1 mg
	Sodium	163 mg
	Fat	.6 g

DROP CHEESE BISCUITS

Speckled with cheese. These are so easy.

All-purpose flour	2 cups	500 mL
Granulated sugar	1 tbsp.	15 mL
Baking powder	4 tsp.	20 mL
Salt	¼ tsp.	1 mL
Grated low-fat sharp Cheddar cheese (less than 21% MF)	1½ cups	375 mL
Vegetable cooking oil	2 tbsp.	30 mL
Skim milk	1 cup	250 mL

(continued on next page)

Measure first 5 ingredients into bowl. Stir.

Add cooking oil and milk. Stir until moistened. Drop by spoonfuls onto baking sheet that has been sprayed with no-stick cooking spray. Bake in 425°F (220°C) oven for about 12 to 15 minutes. Makes 16 biscuits.

Pictured on page 125.

NUTRITION GUIDE	1 biscuit contains:	
	Energy	120 Calories (501 kJ)
	Cholesterol	7 mg
	Sodium	127 mg
	Fat	4.2 g

WHOLE WHEAT BISCUITS

Looks so different from the usual white. So good! They look like little loaves of bread.

Whole wheat flour	2 cups	450 mL
Baking powder	1 tbsp.	15 mL
Salt	1/4 tsp.	1 mL
Vegetable cooking oil	2 tbsp.	30 mL
Mild molasses	1 tbsp.	15 mL
Skim milk	3/4 cup	175 mL

Stir flour, baking powder and salt together in bowl.

Add cooking oil, molasses and milk. Stir to form a soft dough. Knead 8 times on lightly floured surface. Roll or pat 3/4 inch (2 cm) thick. Cut into 1 x 2 inch (2.5 x 5 cm) rectangles. Arrange on ungreased baking sheet. Bake in 425°F (220°C) oven for 12 to 15 minutes. Makes 19 biscuits.

Pictured on page 53.

NUTRITION GUIDE	1 biscuit contains:	
	Energy	65 Calories (272 kJ)
	Cholesterol	trace
	Sodium	44 mg
	Fat	1.7 g

POTATO BISCUITS

Very moist. Serve warm with your favorite casserole.

All-purpose flour	1½ cups	350 mL
Baking powder	1 tbsp.	15 mL
Salt	½ tsp.	2 mL
Granulated sugar	1 tbsp.	15 mL
Skim milk	⅔ cup	150 mL
Cooked mashed potato	1 cup	225 mL
Vegetable cooking oil	3 tbsp.	50 mL

Measure first 4 ingredients into bowl. Stir.

Add remaining ingredients. Stir until soft ball forms. Knead 6 or 8 times on lightly floured surface. Roll out ¾ inch (2 cm) thick. Cut into 2 inch (5 cm) rounds. Arrange on baking sheet sprayed with no-stick cooking spray. Bake in 425°F (220°C) oven for 15 minutes until lightly browned and risen. Makes 16 biscuits.

Pictured on page 17.

NUTRITION GUIDE	1 biscuit contains:	
	Energy	80 Calories (335 kJ)
	Cholesterol	trace
	Sodium	94 mg
	Fat	2.7 g

BRANDIED FRUIT

Be different. Serve this hot thickened fruit with any meat to make the occasion more festive.

Canned unsweetened fruit salad or fruit cocktail with juice	14 oz.	398 mL
Brandy flavoring	1 tsp.	5 mL
Liquid sweetener	1 tbsp.	15 mL
Maple flavoring	¼ tsp.	1 mL
Cornstarch	2 tbsp.	30 mL
Water	2 tbsp.	30 mL

(continued on next page)

Heat first 4 ingredients in saucepan until it boils.

Mix cornstarch in water in small cup. Stir into boiling fruit until it returns to a boil and thickens. Serve hot. Makes $1^{2}/_{3}$ cups (375 mL).

Pictured on page 35.

NUTRITION GUIDE	$^{1}/_{4}$ cup (60 mL) contains:	
	Energy	43 Calories (182 kJ)
	Cholesterol	0 mg
	Sodium	4 mg
	Fat	trace

CORNY BISCUITS

Cornmeal gives these good little biscuits a bit of a crunch.

Cornmeal	$^{3}/_{4}$ **cup**	**175 mL**
Onion flakes	**1 tbsp.**	**15 mL**
Skim milk	$^{3}/_{4}$ **cup**	**175 mL**
Biscuit mix	**2 cups**	**450 mL**

Combine cornmeal, onion flakes and milk in bowl. Let stand 10 minutes.

Add biscuit mix. Stir to form a soft ball of dough. Knead 6 to 8 times. Roll $^{3}/_{4}$ inch (2 cm) thick on lightly floured surface. Cut into 2 inch (5 cm) circles. Arrange on ungreased baking sheet. Bake in 400°F (205°C) oven for 15 minutes or until browned. Makes 15 biscuits.

Pictured on page 71.

NUTRITION GUIDE	1 biscuit contains:	
	Energy	96 Calories (403 kJ)
	Cholesterol	trace
	Sodium	219 mg
	Fat	2.3 g

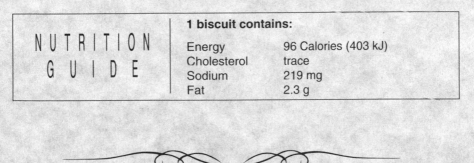

BEET RELISH

Pretty color. Serve with cold or hot meat.

Canned beets, drained, diced or ground	14 oz.	398 mL
Grated cabbage	1 cup	250 mL
Chopped onion	¼ cup	60 mL
Prepared horseradish	¾ tsp.	4 mL
White vinegar	½ cup	125 mL
Salt	½ tsp.	2 mL
Pepper	⅛ tsp.	0.5 mL
Liquid sweetener (or 6 tbsp., 100 mL, granulated sugar)	4 tsp.	20 mL

Combine first 7 ingredients in large pot. Bring to a boil, stirring often. Simmer for 3 minutes. Cool.

Stir in sweetener. Store in refrigerator. Makes 2 cups (450 mL).

NUTRITION GUIDE	1 tbsp. (15 mL) contains:	
	Energy	4 Calories (18 kJ)
	Cholesterol	0 mg
	Sodium	72 mg
	Fat	trace

PASTRY

Cholesterol-free crust.

All-purpose flour	1 cup	250 mL
Vegetable cooking oil	¼ cup	60 mL
Salt	¼ tsp.	1 mL
Water	3 tbsp.	50 mL

Combine all ingredients in bowl. Stir to mix and form a ball. Roll between 2 sheets of waxed paper. Fit into 9 inch (22 cm) pie plate.

NUTRITION GUIDE	⅛ single crust contains:	
	Energy	121 Calories (507 kJ)
	Cholesterol	0 mg
	Sodium	85 mg
	Fat	7 g

LAMB STEAK CASSEROLE

Oranges and juice add a slightly different flavor. Rice is added raw which is a great time saver.

Boneless lamb shoulder steak, trimmed of fat	**1½ lbs.**	**680 g**
Long grain rice, uncooked	**1 cup**	**250 mL**
Canned mandarin oranges, drained, juice reserved	**10 oz.**	**284 mL**
Reserved orange juice plus boiling water to make	**3 cups**	**750 mL**
Beef bouillon powder (35% less salt)	**4 tsp.**	**20 mL**

Spray hot frying pan with no-stick cooking spray. Add lamb steak. Brown both sides. Place in 2 quart (2 L) casserole.

Pour rice evenly over top followed by orange segments.

Stir juice-water mixture with bouillon to dissolve. Pour over casserole. Cover. Bake in 325°F (160°C) oven for 1¼ to 1¾ hours until rice is cooked and meat is tender. Makes 6 servings.

NUTRITION GUIDE	1 serving contains:	
	Energy	268 Calories (1122 kJ)
	Cholesterol	74 mg
	Sodium	245 mg
	Fat	6.4 g

BEEF STEAK CASSEROLE: Use beef instead of lamb.

Old used batteries don't cost anything. They're free of charge.

LAMB CREOLE

Just the right blend of spices.

Boneless lamb, cubed, trimmed of fat	2 lbs.	900 g
Sliced fresh mushrooms	2 cups	500 mL
Canned tomatoes, broken up	14 oz.	398 mL
Red wine (or alcohol-free red wine)	1 cup	250 mL
Sliced onion	1 cup	250 mL
Green pepper, seeded and cut in slivers	1	1
Bay leaf	1	1
Salt	¾ tsp.	4 mL
Pepper	¼ tsp.	1 mL
Thyme	¼ tsp.	1 mL
Garlic powder	¼ tsp.	1 mL

Combine all ingredients in 3 quart (3 L) casserole. Stir well. Cover. Bake in 325°F (160°C) oven for 3 hours until meat is tender. Discard bay leaf. Makes 8 servings.

NUTRITION GUIDE	1 serving contains:	
	Energy	178 Calories (745 kJ)
	Cholesterol	73 mg
	Sodium	385 mg
	Fat	6 g

BEEF CREOLE: Use beef instead of lamb.

1. Chicken Rice Bake page 61
2. Green Chili Quiche page 150
3. Pork Casserole page 123
4. Tomato Scallop page 142

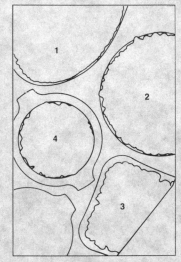

Colorful with a mild taste similar to lasagne. Lean ground beef may be used instead of lamb.

Lean ground leg of lamb	1 lb.	454 g
Finely chopped onion	½ cup	125 mL
Canned tomatoes	14 oz.	398 mL
Garlic powder	¼ tsp.	1 mL
Salt	½ tsp.	2 mL
Pepper	¼ tsp.	1 mL
Granulated sugar	½ tsp.	2 mL
Sliced carrots	1½ cups	375 mL
Boiling water		
Dry colored fusilli (or other pasta)	2⅔ cups	600 mL
Boiling water	3 qts.	3 L
Low-fat plain yogurt (less than 1% MF)	1 cup	250 mL
Low-fat cottage cheese (less than 1% MF)	1 cup	250 mL
All-purpose flour	2 tbsp.	30 mL
Parsley flakes	2 tsp.	10 mL
Grated low-fat sharp Cheddar cheese (less than 21% MF)	1 cup	250 mL

Spray frying pan with no-stick vegetable spray. Add ground lamb and onion. Sauté until browned and onion is soft.

Add next 5 ingredients. Stir.

Cook carrots in some boiling water until tender. Drain.

Cook fusilli in second amount of boiling water in large uncovered pot about 10 minutes until tender but firm. Drain. Add carrots.

Stir yogurt, cottage cheese, flour and parsley together well. Add to fusilli. Stir. Place ½ meat mixture in 3 quart (3 L) casserole followed by ½ noodle mixture, second ½ meat and second ½ noodles. Cover. Bake in 350°F (175°C) oven for 25 to 30 minutes.

Sprinkle with cheese. Bake for 5 to 8 minutes more until cheese melts. Makes 8¼ cups (1.85L).

Pictured on cover.

NUTRITION GUIDE	1 cup (225 mL) contains:	
	Energy	296 Calories (1237 kJ)
	Cholesterol	44 mg
	Sodium	532 mg
	Fat	6.5 g

MOUSSAKA

Sweet spices are added to this Greek dish.

Medium eggplants, cut ½ inch (12 mm) thick	2	2
Chopped onion	2 cups	500 mL
Lean ground leg of lamb	1½ lbs.	680 g
Tomato paste	2 tbsp.	30 mL
Salt	1 tsp.	5 mL
Pepper	½ tsp.	2 mL
Garlic powder	¼ tsp.	1 mL
Cinnamon	¼ tsp.	1 mL
Parsley flakes	1 tsp.	5 mL
Water	½ cup	125 mL
CREAM SAUCE		
All-purpose flour	¼ cup	60 mL
Salt	½ tsp.	2 mL
Pepper	¼ tsp.	1 mL
Nutmeg	⅛ tsp.	0.5 mL
Skim milk	2 cups	450 mL
Low-fat cottage cheese (less than 1% MF), mashed with fork	1 cup	225 mL
Grated Parmesan cheese	½ cup	125 mL

Broil eggplant to cook and brown both sides.

Spray frying pan with no-stick cooking spray. Add onion. Sauté until soft and clear. Transfer to bowl.

Spray frying pan again. Add ground lamb. Scramble-fry until no pink remains in meat. Remove from heat.

Add next 7 ingredients to meat. Add onion. Stir.

(continued on next page)

Cream Sauce: Combine flour, salt, pepper and nutmeg in saucepan. Add a bit of milk and stir until no lumps remain. Add rest of milk. Heat and stir until it boils and thickens. Remove from heat.

Stir in cottage cheese. Layer in 9 x 13 inch (22 x 33 cm) pan:

1. ½ eggplant slices
2. ½ meat sauce
3. ⅓ Parmesan cheese
4. ½ eggplant slices
5. ½ meat sauce
6. ⅓ Parmesan cheese
7. All Cream Sauce
8. ⅓ Parmesan cheese

Bake, uncovered, in 350°F (175°C) oven for about 45 minutes until golden. Cut into 12 squares.

NUTRITION GUIDE	1 square contains:	
	Energy	156 Calories (652 kJ)
	Cholesterol	40 mg
	Sodium	564 mg
	Fat	4.8 g

Variation: Use beef instead of lamb.

Policemen who play tennis belong to the racket squad.

MEAL IN A DISH

Everything is mixed together raw. Lean ground beef may be used instead of lamb.

Chopped onion	1½ cups	375 mL
Frozen kernel corn	1 cup	250 mL
Grated carrot, packed	1 cup	250 mL
All-purpose flour	¼ cup	60 mL
Salt	1 tsp.	5 mL
Pepper	¼ tsp.	1 mL
Canned tomatoes	14 oz.	398 mL
Lean ground leg of lamb	1 lb.	454 g
Worcestershire sauce	1 tsp.	5 mL
Medium potatoes, peeled and cubed	4	4

Combine first 6 ingredients in large bowl. Stir well until flour is evenly mixed.

Add tomatoes, ground lamb and Worcestershire sauce. Mix.

Stir in potatoes. Turn into 3 quart (3 L) casserole. Cover. Bake in 350°F (175°C) oven for about 2 hours until potatoes are tender and meat is cooked. Makes about 7 cups (1.6 L).

NUTRITION GUIDE	1 cup (225 mL) contains:	
	Energy	213 Calories (893 kJ)
	Cholesterol	40 mg
	Sodium	541 mg
	Fat	4 g

Variation: Use beef instead of lamb.

Habits can be harmful. The carpenter broke his teeth by biting his nails.

Could be Irish Stew.

Lamb cubes, from neck or shoulder	1 lb.	454 g
Peeled cubed potatoes	2 cups	500 mL
Chopped onion	1 cup	250 mL
Sliced celery	1 cup	250 mL
Green pepper, seeded, cut in short slivers	1	1
Boiling water	1½ cups	375 mL
Beef bouillon powder (35% less salt)	4 tsp.	20 mL
Frozen peas	2 cups	500 mL

Spray frying pan with no-stick cooking spray. Add lamb. Brown. Turn into 2 quart (2 L) casserole.

Add next 4 ingredients.

Mix water with bouillon powder. Pour into frying pan, loosen brown bits and pour over lamb. Cover. Bake in 350°F (175°C) oven for 1½ hours.

Add peas. Stir lightly. Continue to bake for 15 minutes until peas are cooked and meat is tender. Makes 6 cups (1.35 L).

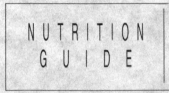

N U T R I T I O N
G U I D E

1 cup (225 mL) contains:	
Energy	210 Calories (878 kJ)
Cholesterol	49 mg
Sodium	296 mg
Fat	4.5 g

BEEF DINNER DISH: Use beef instead of lamb.

After he was made a ruler, he was the straightest man around.

PINEAPPLE HAM PIZZA

This has a rice crust covered with cheese, ham and pineapple.

RICE CRUST

Long grain rice	½ cup	125 mL
Boiling water	1 cup	250 mL
All-purpose flour	1½ cups	350 mL
Fast rising instant yeast	1½ tsp.	7 mL
Warm water	½ cup	125 mL

TOPPING

Tomato paste	½ × 5½ oz.	½ × 156 mL
Water	⅓ cup	75 mL
Onion powder	¼ tsp.	1 mL
Oregano	¼ tsp.	1 mL
Liquid sweetener	¼ tsp.	1 mL
Basil	¼ tsp.	1 mL
Garlic salt	½ tsp.	2 mL
Grated part-skim mozzarella cheese (35% less fat)	¾ cup	175 mL
Unsweetened pineapple tidbits, drained	14 oz.	398 mL
Ham cubes	⅔ cup	150 mL
Green pepper, seeded and cut in slivers	½	½
Grated part-skim mozzarella cheese (35% less fat)	¾ cup	175 mL
Grated low-fat medium or sharp Cheddar cheese (less than 21% MF)	½ cup	125 mL

Rice Crust: Cook rice in boiling water until tender and water is absorbed. Measure 1¼ cups (275 mL) into bowl. Cool a little.

Add flour and yeast. Stir well. Add water. Mix. Knead 25 times on lightly floured surface mixing in a bit more flour if sticky. Roll and stretch to fit 12 inch (30 cm) pizza pan that has been sprayed with no-stick cooking spray.

(continued on next page)

Topping: Stir first 7 ingredients together. Spread over crust.

Sprinkle with first amount of mozzarella cheese, pineapple, ham and green pepper. Bake on bottom shelf of 450°F (230°C) oven for 20 minutes.

Sprinkle with second amount of mozzarella cheese. Add Cheddar cheese. Continue to bake for 5 to 10 minutes more until cheese is melted and crust is browned. Cut into 8 wedges.

Pictured on page 53.

N U T R I T I O N G U I D E	1 wedge contains:	
	Energy	241 Calories (1009 kJ)
	Cholesterol	22 mg
	Sodium	400 mg
	Fat	5.9 g

SWEET AND SOUR HAM BALLS

Amazing morsels. Great for company.

Lean ground cooked ham	1 lb.	454 g
Lean ground pork	1 lb.	454 g
Dry fine bread crumbs	2 cups	500 mL
Skim milk	1 cup	250 mL
All-purpose flour	1/4 cup	60 mL
Dry mustard powder	1 tsp.	5 mL
Brown sugar	1 1/2 cups	350 mL
White vinegar	3/4 cup	175 mL
Water	3/4 cup	175 mL
Pineapple or orange juice	3/4 cup	175 mL

In large bowl mix first 4 ingredients together well. Shape into 1 inch (2.5 cm) balls. Place on shallow baking sheet. Bake, uncovered, in 375°F (190°C) oven for 20 minutes. Drain. Place in 3 quart (3 L) casserole.

Mix flour, mustard and brown sugar in small saucepan. Stir in remaining ingredients until it boils and thickens. Pour over meatballs. Bake, uncovered, for another 20 minutes. Makes 84 meatballs. Serves 12.

N U T R I T I O N G U I D E	1 serving (7 meatballs) contains:	
	Energy	241 Calories (1008 kJ)
	Cholesterol	30 mg
	Sodium	650 mg
	Fat	3.5 g

HAM PASTA CASSEROLE

Creamy yellow in color. The ham and tomato add even more color to this tasty dish.

Chopped onion	½ cup	125 mL
Dry elbow macaroni	2 cups	500 mL
Boiling water	3 qts.	3 L
Grated low-fat sharp Cheddar cheese (less than 21% MF)	¾ cup	175 mL
Lean cooked ham slice, cubed (¼ lb., 125 g)	¾ cup	175 mL
Medium tomatoes, diced	2	2
Condensed cream of chicken soup	10 oz.	284 mL
Skim milk	½ cup	125 mL
Prepared mustard	1 tsp.	5 mL

Cook onion and macaroni in boiling water in large uncovered saucepan until macaroni is tender but firm. Drain. Return to saucepan.

Add cheese, ham and tomato.

In bowl whisk soup, milk and mustard together. Stir into macaroni mixture. Turn into 2 quart (2 L) casserole. Bake, uncovered, in 350°F (175°C) oven for 20 minutes until quite hot. Makes 6⅓ cups (1.43 L).

NUTRITION GUIDE	1 cup (225 mL) contains:	
	Energy	259 Calories (1085 kJ)
	Cholesterol	21 mg
	Sodium	735 mg
	Fat	7.0 g

Incredibly good. The stuffing makes them taste like more.

STUFFING

Chopped onion	1/3 cup	75 mL
Chopped celery	2 tbsp.	30 mL
Water	1/2 cup	125 mL
Dry bread crumbs	2 cups	500 mL
Parsley flakes	1 tsp.	5 mL
Poultry seasoning	3/4 tsp.	4 mL
Salt	1/4 tsp.	1 mL
Pepper	1/8 tsp.	0.5 mL
Water	1 cup	250 mL
Lean cooked ham slices (see Note)	16	16
Paprika, sprinkle		
Grated low-fat sharp or medium Cheddar cheese (less than 21% MF)	3 tbsp.	50 mL

Stuffing: Cook onion and celery in first amount of water until soft. Do not drain.

Add bread crumbs, parsley, poultry seasoning, salt, pepper and second amount of water. Stir well. Add more water as needed so it will hold together.

Place 2 tbsp. (30 mL) filling down center of each ham slice. Roll. Place seam side down in 9 x 13 inch (22 x 33 cm) pan, making 2 long rows side by side.

Sprinkle with paprika. Cover. Bake in 350°F (175°C) oven for 20 minutes.

Sprinkle cheese down center of each row. Cover. Bake 5 minutes more. Makes 16 rolls.

Note: Square cooked ham slices, 6 per 6 oz. (175 g) package, were used for this recipe.

NUTRITION GUIDE	1 roll contains:	
	Energy	100 Calories (416 kJ)
	Cholesterol	14 mg
	Sodium	564 mg
	Fat	2.4 g

ZUCCHINI PORK BAKE

So colorful with green and orange showing through the top.

Lean ground pork	1 lb.	454 g
Salt	$\frac{1}{2}$ tsp.	2 mL
Onion powder	$\frac{1}{4}$ tsp.	1 mL
Sage	$\frac{1}{8}$ tsp.	0.5 mL
Thyme	$\frac{1}{8}$ tsp.	0.5 mL
Pepper	$\frac{1}{8}$ tsp.	0.5 mL
Zucchini with peel, cubed, about 1$\frac{1}{4}$ lbs. (570 g)	4 cups	900 mL
Water		
Sweet potato, peeled and cubed	2 cups	450 mL
Water		
Frozen egg product, thawed, (low-fat and cholesterol-free)	$\frac{1}{2}$ cup	125 mL
Egg white (large)	1	1
Cracker crumbs (unsalted)	$\frac{1}{4}$ cup	60 mL
Grated low-fat sharp Cheddar cheese (less than 21% MF)	$\frac{1}{2}$ cup	125 mL

Spray frying pan with no-stick cooking spray. Add ground pork. Scramble-fry. Mix in next 5 ingredients.

Cook zucchini in some water until tender crisp. Drain.

Cook sweet potato in some water until tender crisp. Drain.

Combine egg product, egg white, cracker crumbs and cheese in large bowl. Add ground pork, zucchini and sweet potato. Toss lightly to distribute evenly. Turn into 2 quart (2 L) casserole. Cover. Bake, in 350°F (175°C) oven for about 30 minutes. Makes 6$\frac{1}{2}$ cups (1.5 L).

N U T R I T I O N G U I D E	1 cup (225 mL) contains:	
	Energy	182 Calories (760 kJ)
	Cholesterol	28 mg
	Sodium	379 mg
	Fat	4.2 g

Breakfast in a pan.

SAUCE

All-purpose flour	2 tbsp.	30 mL
Salt	$\frac{1}{4}$ tsp.	1 mL
Pepper	$\frac{1}{8}$ tsp.	0.5 mL
Skim milk	1 cup	250 mL
Sliced green onion	2 tbsp.	30 mL
Sliced fresh small mushrooms	1 cup	250 mL
Frozen egg product, thawed (low-fat and cholesterol-free	1$\frac{1}{2}$ cups	375 mL
Egg whites (large)	2	2
Medium potatoes, cooked, peeled and grated	2	2
Lean ham cubes	$\frac{1}{2}$ cup	125 mL

TOPPING

Hard margarine, melted	1 tbsp.	15 mL
Dry bread crumbs	$\frac{1}{2}$ cup	125 mL
Water	1 tbsp.	15 mL

Sauce: Combine flour, salt and pepper in saucepan. Whisk in milk gradually until smooth. Heat and stir until it boils and thickens.

Spray frying pan with no-stick cooking spray. Add onion and mushrooms. Sauté until soft. Add to sauce.

Spray frying pan again. Add egg product and egg whites. Scramble-fry until cooked. Stir into sauce.

Add potato and ham. Stir. Turn into 9 x 9 inch (22 x 22 cm) pan which has been sprayed with no-stick cooking spray.

Topping: Stir all 3 ingredients together well. Sprinkle over top. Bake in 350°F (175°C) oven for about 40 minutes. Cut into 9 squares.

N U T R I T I O N
G U I D E

1 square contains:

Energy	119 Calories (498 kJ)
Cholesterol	4 mg
Sodium	354 mg
Fat	2.4 g

HAM SCALLOP

Good flavor. A green salad complements this dish.

Lean ham slice, about ½ inch (12 mm) thick, cubed or slivered	1 lb.	454 g
Potatoes, peeled and thinly sliced	2 lbs.	900 g
Cauliflower florets	1 cup	250 mL
Chopped or sliced onion	1 cup	250 mL
Peas, fresh or frozen	1 cup	250 mL
SAUCE		
All-purpose flour	⅓ cup	75 mL
Pepper	¼ tsp.	1 mL
Cayenne pepper	⅛ tsp.	0.5 mL
Parsley flakes	½ tsp.	2 mL
Skim milk	2½ cups	575 mL

Put first 5 ingredients into large bowl.

Sauce: Stir flour, pepper, cayenne pepper and parsley together in saucepan. Whisk in part of the milk until no lumps remain. Whisk in rest of milk. Heat and stir on medium-high until it boils and thickens. Pour over contents in bowl. Stir. Pour into 3 quart (3 L) casserole. Cover. Bake in 350°F (175°C) oven for about 60 minutes until potato is tender. Makes 9 cups (2 L).

NUTRITION GUIDE	1 cup (225 mL) contains:	
	Energy	221 Calories (924 kJ)
	Cholesterol	24 mg
	Sodium	706 mg
	Fat	2.6 g

PORK CHOP BAKE

Fantastic flavor in both meat and gravy.

Boneless pork chops, fat removed	2 lbs.	900 g
Condensed cream of mushroom soup	10 oz.	284 mL
White wine (or alcohol-free wine)	¼ cup	60 mL
Beef bouillon powder (35% less salt)	2 tsp.	10 mL
Onion flakes	1 tbsp.	15 mL

(continued on next page)

Arrange pork chops in 3 quart (3 L) casserole.

Mix remaining ingredients in small bowl. Spoon over and between pork chops. Cover. Bake in 350°F (175°C) oven for 1½ hours or until very tender. Makes 8 servings.

N U T R I T I O N G U I D E	**1 serving contains:**	
	Energy	131 Calories (550 kJ)
	Cholesterol	37 mg
	Sodium	413 mg
	Fat	5.4 g

PORK POT

Pork and vegetables with a stroganoff gravy.

Lean pork, cut bite size	**1 lb.**	**454 g**
Sliced carrots	**1½ cups**	**375 mL**
Peeled sliced potatoes	**2 cups**	**500 mL**
Chopped onion	**⅓ cup**	**75 mL**
Low-fat sour cream (7% MF)	**1 cup**	**250 mL**
Water	**1 cup**	**250 mL**
Beef bouillon powder (35% less salt)	**4 tsp.**	**20 mL**

Spray frying pan with no-stick cooking spray. Add pork. Sauté to brown well. Turn into 2 quart (2 L) casserole.

Add carrots, potatoes and onion.

Stir sour cream, water and bouillon powder together in frying pan to loosen brown bits. Pour into casserole. Stir lightly. Cover. Bake in 350°F (175°C) oven for about 1½ hours until meat and vegetables are tender. Makes 5 cups (1.13 L).

N U T R I T I O N G U I D E	**1 cup (225 mL) contains:**	
	Energy	206 Calories (860 kJ)
	Cholesterol	39 mg
	Sodium	332 mg
	Fat	5.8 g

VERY FIRST RIBS

Fantastic. Served with a dark reddish sauce. Pre-boiling ribs reduces fat content.

Lean meaty pork back ribs	4 lbs.	1.82 kg
Water to cover		
Water	1 cup	250 mL
Chopped onion	½ cup	125 mL
White vinegar	¾ cup	175 mL
Worcestershire sauce	2 tbsp.	30 mL
Granulated sugar	½ cup	125 mL
Dry mustard	1 tsp.	5 mL
Salt	1½ tsp.	7 mL
Pepper	¼ tsp.	1 mL
Ground cloves	⅛ tsp.	0.5 mL
Tomato paste	5½ oz.	156 mL

Cut ribs into 2 rib servings. Place in large pot. Add water. Cover. Bring to a boil. Boil for 30 minutes. Drain.

Measure remaining ingredients into saucepan. Heat, stirring frequently until it simmers. Simmer gently until onion is soft. Using tongs, transfer ribs to roaster. Pour sauce over top. Cover. Bake in 350°F (175°C) oven for 1 hour. Makes 8 servings.

Pictured on page 125.

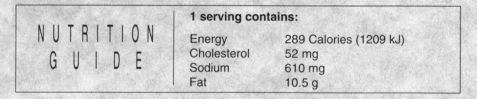

NUTRITION GUIDE	1 serving contains:	
	Energy	289 Calories (1209 kJ)
	Cholesterol	52 mg
	Sodium	610 mg
	Fat	10.5 g

If you are hired to make a bandstand, just take away all the chairs.

Apples lend a different flavor while carrots add color.

Lean pork steaks, fat removed, cut bite size	1½ lbs.	680 g
Chopped onion	2 cups	500 mL
Bite size carrot chunks	2 cups	500 mL
Peeled, chopped and cored apple	2 cups	500 mL
All-purpose flour	3 tbsp.	50 mL
Chicken bouillon powder (35% less salt)	1 tbsp.	15 mL
Pepper	¼ tsp.	1 mL
Water	2 cups	500 mL
Gravy browner as needed	¼ tsp.	1 mL

Spray frying pan with no-stick cooking spray. Brown steaks.

Combine pork, onion, carrot and apple in 3 quart (3 L) casserole.

Stir flour, bouillon powder and pepper in saucepan. Mix in a small amount of water until no lumps remain. Add rest of water. Add a bit of gravy browner to make a richer color. Heat and stir until it boils and thickens. Pour over casserole. Cover. Bake in 350°F (175°C) oven for about 2 hours until vegetables and meat are tender. Makes 6 servings.

Pictured on page 107.

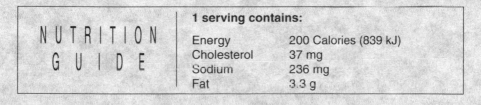

NUTRITION GUIDE	**1 serving contains:**	
	Energy	200 Calories (839 kJ)
	Cholesterol	37 mg
	Sodium	236 mg
	Fat	3.3 g

Chicken noodle is actually a cowardly pasta soup.

WIENER PASTA BAKE

Pasta is added raw. Convenient and very good.

Condensed tomato soup	2 × 10 oz.	2 × 284 mL
Boiling water	2½ cups	625 mL
Chili powder	2 tsp.	10 mL
Small fresh mushrooms (slice bigger ones)	1½ cups	375 mL
Dry elbow macaroni	2 cups	500 mL
Wieners, cut in 6 pieces each	1 lb.	454 g

Mix soup, water and chili powder in 3 quart (3 L) casserole until smooth.

Add remaining ingredients. Stir. Cover. Bake in 350°F (175°C) oven for about 45 to 60 minutes until macaroni is tender. Makes 8 servings.

Pictured on page 17.

NUTRITION GUIDE	1 serving contains:	
	Energy	343 Calories (1435 kJ)
	Cholesterol	28 mg
	Sodium	1167 mg
	Fat	18.3 g

1. Very First Ribs page 122
2. Drop Cheese Biscuits page 100
3. Teener's Dish page 19
4. Chicken Cola page 70

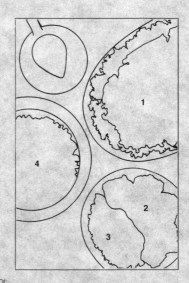

Dishes Courtesy Of:
The Bay Housewares Dept.

Background Courtesy Of:
Chintz & Company

PORK CHOPS SUPREME

Delicious casserole. Chops with mushrooms, onion and gravy.

Boneless pork chops, fat removed, 2 lbs. (900 g)	**8**	**8**
Skim milk	**1 cup**	**250 mL**
Water	**²/₃ cup**	**150 mL**
All-purpose flour	**¼ cup**	**60 mL**
Parsley flakes	**½ tsp.**	**2 mL**
Garlic powder	**¼ tsp.**	**1 mL**
Beef bouillon powder (35% less salt)	**1 tsp.**	**5 mL**
Water	**6 tbsp.**	**100 mL**
Chopped fresh mushrooms	**2 cups**	**500 mL**
Chopped onion	**1 cup**	**250 mL**

Spray hot frying pan with no-stick cooking spray. Brown chops on both sides. Remove to plate.

Add milk and first amount of water to frying pan. Stir to loosen brown bits.

Stir next 4 ingredients together in bowl. Mix in remaining water until no lumps remain. Stir into liquid until it boils and thickens.

Add mushrooms and onion. Arrange pork chops in 3 quart (3 L) casserole spooning sauce between and over top. Cover. Bake in 350°F (175°C) oven for 1½ hours or until tender. Makes 8 servings.

Pictured on page 71.

NUTRITION GUIDE	**1 serving contains:**	
	Energy	129 Calories (541 kJ)
	Cholesterol	37 mg
	Sodium	90 mg
	Fat	2.8 g

SPECIAL DAY RIBS

These are dressed up with fruit. Excellent sweet and sour flavor. Pre-boiling reduces fat.

Lean meaty pork back ribs	4 lbs.	1.82 kg
Water to cover		
White vinegar	¼ cup	60 mL
Light soy sauce (40% less salt)	¼ cup	60 mL
Reserved juice from pineapple		
Reserved juice from apricots		
Chopped onion	⅔ cup	150 mL
Garlic powder (or 1 clove minced)	¼ tsp.	1 mL
Brown sugar, packed	½ cup	125 mL
Liquid sweetener	1 tbsp.	15 mL
Cornstarch	2 tbsp.	30 mL
Water	2 tbsp.	30 mL
Canned unsweetened pineapple tidbits, drained, juice reserved	14 oz.	398 mL
Canned unsweetened apricots, drained, juice reserved	14 oz.	398 mL

Cut ribs into 2-rib portions. Boil in water for 30 minutes. Drain. Place in roaster.

Combine next 8 ingredients in saucepan. Stir. Bring to a boil.

Mix cornstarch and water together in small cup. Stir into boiling liquid until it boils and thickens.

Pour sauce over ribs. Cover. Cook in 350°F (175°C) oven for 1 hour. Spoon drained fruit over ribs. Cover and cook 15 minutes more. Makes 8 servings.

Pictured on page 35.

NUTRITION GUIDE	1 serving contains:	
	Energy	339 Calories (1420 kJ)
	Cholesterol	52 mg
	Sodium	361 mg
	Fat	10.3 g

Variation: If you aren't watching sugar intake, omit sweetener and add 1 cup (250 mL) brown sugar. Of course it's delicious.

Scrumptious rolls stuffed with a mild curried rice covered with a curried raisin sauce.

Long grain rice	**½ cup**	**125 mL**
Boiling water	**1 cup**	**250 mL**
Finely chopped onion	**1 tbsp.**	**15 mL**
Parsley flakes	**½ tsp.**	**2 mL**
CURRY SAUCE		
All-purpose flour	**4 tbsp.**	**60 mL**
Curry powder	**¾ tsp.**	**4 mL**
Salt	**½ tsp.**	**2 mL**
Skim milk	**2 cups**	**450 mL**
Raisins	**¾ cup**	**175 mL**
Prepared rice		
Prepared sauce	**½ cup**	**125 mL**
Lean ham slices (see Note)	**16**	**16**

Cook rice in water about 15 minutes until tender and water is absorbed.

Stir in onion and parsley.

Curry Sauce: Measure flour, curry powder and salt into saucepan. Whisk in enough milk to mix until no lumps remain. Add rest of milk and raisins. Heat and stir until it boils and thickens.

Stir rice and ½ cup (125 mL) sauce together.

Place 2 tbsp. (30 mL) rice mixture down center of ham. Roll. Place seam side down in 9 x 13 inch (22 x 33 cm) pan, making 2 long rows side by side. Spoon remaining sauce over top. Cover. Bake in 350°F (175°C) oven for about 20 minutes until hot. Makes 16 rolls.

Note: Square cooked ham slices, 6 per 6 oz. (175 g) package, were used for this recipe.

Pictured on page 17.

NUTRITION GUIDE	1 roll contains:	
	Energy	94 Calories (393 kJ)
	Cholesterol	14 mg
	Sodium	508 mg
	Fat	1.6 g

HAM ASPARAGUS BAKE

Serve with mashed potatoes and a salad and you will have a real hit.

All-purpose flour	**3 tbsp.**	**50 mL**
Salt	**¼ tsp.**	**1 mL**
Pepper	**⅛ tsp.**	**0.5 mL**
Skim milk	**1⅓ cups**	**300 mL**
Cubed cooked lean ham	**1 cup**	**250 mL**
Onion powder	**¼ tsp.**	**1 mL**
Frozen asparagus spears, cut in 1 inch (2.5 cm) lengths	**10 oz.**	**284 g**
Boiling water		
Sesame seeds, toasted in 350°F (175°) oven, about 5 minutes	**1½ tsp.**	**7 mL**

Measure flour, salt and pepper in saucepan. Whisk in part of milk until no lumps remain. Add rest of milk. Heat and stir until it boils and thickens.

Stir in ham and onion powder. Remove from heat.

Cook asparagus in some boiling water until tender. Drain. Add to ham mixture. Stir lightly. Turn into 1½ quart (1.5 L) casserole.

Sprinkle with sesame seeds. Bake, uncovered, in 350°F (175°C) oven for 20 to 25 minutes. Makes 6 servings.

HAM CAULIFLOWER BAKE: Add about 1 lb. (454 g) cooked cauliflower instead of asparagus. Excellent combination.

Paré Pointer

Ships carry most vegetables in their dining room, except leeks that is.

You will hesitate to take out the first spoonful from this picturesque dish.

Grated peeled potato (1 medium)	1 cup	250 mL
Chopped onion	¼ cup	60 mL
Chopped green pepper	¼ cup	60 mL
Chopped mushrooms	1 cup	250 mL
Skim milk	⅔ cup	150 mL
All-purpose flour	⅔ cup	150 mL
Chicken bouillon powder (less than 35% salt)	1 tsp.	5 mL
Paprika	⅛ tsp.	0.5 mL
Cayenne pepper	⅛ tsp.	0.5 mL
Skim milk	2 cups	500 mL
Lean diced ham (about 9 oz., 255 g)	1½ cups	350 mL
CHEESE BISCUITS		
All-purpose flour	1½ cups	350 mL
Baking powder	2½ tsp.	12 mL
Grated low-fat sharp Cheddar cheese (less than (21% MF)	⅓ cup	75 mL
Vegetable cooking oil	2 tbsp.	30 mL
Skim milk	⅔ cup	150 mL

Spray saucepan with no-stick cooking spray. Add potato, onion, green pepper and mushrooms. Sauté until soft. Set aside.

Whisk first amount of milk with flour, bouillon powder, paprika and cayenne pepper in saucepan until smooth. Add second amount of milk. Heat and stir until it boils and thickens. Stir into onion mixture.

Add ham. Stir. Turn into 2 quart (2 L) casserole. Place in 425°F (220°C) oven to heat while making biscuit topping.

Cheese Biscuits: Stir first 3 ingredients together in bowl.

Add cooking oil and milk. Mix until it forms a soft ball. Roll out ½ inch (12 mm) thick on lightly floured surface. Cut with doughnut cutter. Arrange on top of casserole with small center rounds still in place. Bake, uncovered, for about 15 minutes until browned. Makes 6 servings.

NUTRITION GUIDE	1 serving contains:	
	Energy	357 Calories (1492 kJ)
	Cholesterol	25 mg
	Sodium	707 mg
	Fat	8.5 g

BARBECUED PORK CHOPS

Tomato ketchup flavor with onion and mushrooms.

Boneless loin pork chops, all fat removed, about 4 oz. (114 g) each	**8**	**8**
SAUCE		
Tomato paste	**½ cup**	**125 mL**
White vinegar	**⅔ cup**	**150 mL**
Salt	**½ tsp.**	**2 mL**
Ground cloves	**⅛ tsp.**	**0.5 mL**
Liquid sweetener	**3 tbsp.**	**45 mL**
Prepared mustard	**1 tbsp.**	**15 mL**
Sliced fresh mushrooms	**2 cups**	**500 mL**
Chopped onion	**2 cups**	**500 mL**

Spray frying pan with no-stick cooking spray. Brown pork chops on both sides.

Sauce: Stir next 6 ingredients in medium saucepan. Heat until it boils.

Add mushrooms and onion. Arrange pork chops in small roaster or large casserole, spooning sauce between and over chops. Cover. Bake in 350°F (175°C) oven for about 1½ hours. Makes 8 servings.

N U T R I T I O N G U I D E	**1 serving contains:**	
	Energy	230 Calories (963 kJ)
	Cholesterol	51 mg
	Sodium	264 mg
	Fat	10 g

Give a banana a suntan and it peels.

A lean bean dish.

Dried white beans	**2 cups**	**450 mL**
Water	**6 cups**	**1.5 L**
Chopped onion	**1 cup**	**250 mL**
Molasses	**2 tbsp.**	**30 mL**
Prepared mustard	**1 tsp.**	**5 mL**
Salt	**$\frac{1}{2}$ tsp.**	**2 mL**
Water	**$3\frac{1}{2}$ cups**	**800 mL**
Liquid sweetener	**1 tsp.**	**5 mL**
Liquid smoke	**$\frac{1}{2}$ tsp.**	**2 mL**
Maple flavoring	**$\frac{1}{16}$ tsp.**	**0.5 mL**

Combine beans and first amount of water in large pot. Bring to a boil. Boil for 3 minutes. Remove from heat. Cover. Let stand 1 hour. Drain.

Add next 8 ingredients. Stir. Bring to a boil. Cover. Simmer for about 1 hour. Turn into 2 quart (2 L) casserole or bean pot. Cover. Bake in 300°F (150°C) oven for about 2 hours until tender. Makes 4½ cups (1 L).

N U T R I T I O N G U I D E	**1 cup (225 mL) contains:**	
	Energy	156 Calories (653 kJ)
	Cholesterol	0 mg
	Sodium	328 mg
	Fat	trace

A rolling stone may not gather moss but it squashes bugs.

BAKED SHELF BEANS

These doctored-up beans make a quick change.

Baked beans in tomato sauce	2 x 14 oz.	2 x 398 mL
Onion flakes	3 tbsp.	50 mL
Ketchup, page 99	1 tbsp.	15 mL
Prepared mustard	1 tsp.	5 mL
Mild molasses	1 tbsp.	15 mL
Liquid sweetener	1/2 tsp.	2 mL
Maple flavoring	1/8 tsp.	0.5 mL
Worcestershire sauce	1/2 tsp.	2 mL

Combine all ingredients in large bowl. Stir well to distribute every-thing evenly. Turn into 1 quart (1 L) casserole. Bake, uncovered, in 350°F (175°C) oven for about 1 hour, stirring twice during baking. Makes 3 cups (675 mL).

NUTRITION GUIDE	1/2 cup (125 mL) contains:	
	Energy	155 Calories (650 kJ)
	Cholesterol	0 mg
	Sodium	602 mg
	Fat	.7 g

ASPARAGUS PUFF

Light and good flavor.

Medium potatoes, peeled and quartered	2	2
Water		
Frozen asparagus, chopped	10 oz.	284 g
Water		
All-purpose flour	1 tbsp.	15 mL
Green onions, sliced	2	2
Grated Parmesan cheese	1/4 cup	60 mL
Prepared mustard	1 tsp.	5 mL
Salt	1/2 tsp.	2 mL
Pepper	1/8 tsp.	0.5 mL
Egg whites (large), room temperature	2	2

(continued on next page)

Cook potatoes in some water until tender. Drain. Mash.

Cook asparagus in some water until tender. Drain. Add to potato.

Add next 6 ingredients. Mix.

Beat egg whites in small mixing bowl until stiff. Fold into asparagus mixture. Turn into 1 quart (1 L) casserole. Bake in 350°F (175°C) oven for about 25 minutes until an inserted knife comes out clean. Makes 2½ cups (575 mL).

NUTRITION GUIDE	½ cup (125 mL) contains:	
	Energy	100 Calories (417 kJ)
	Cholesterol	4 mg
	Sodium	408 mg
	Fat	1.8 g

OVEN FRIES

If you have never tried using sweet potatoes, you will enjoy this method. Regular potatoes may be used.

Sweet potatoes, peeled	1½ lbs.	680 g
Vegetable cooking oil	1 tbsp.	15 mL

Cut potatoes into sticks. Place in bowl.

Add cooking oil, tossing to coat. Arrange in single layer on baking sheet that has been sprayed with no-stick cooking spray. Bake in 450°F (230°C) oven for 15 minutes. Turn and bake 10 to 15 minutes more. Makes 4 servings.

NUTRITION GUIDE	1 serving contains:	
	Energy	209 Calories (875 kJ)
	Cholesterol	0 mg
	Sodium	22 mg
	Fat	4 g

Variation: Omit vegetable cooking oil. Toss potatoes as you spray them with no-stick cooking spray. No cholesterol, low in calories and sodium and only a trace of fat.

CHEESY RICE CASSEROLE

Green chilies add zip to the rice.

Long grain rice	1 cup	250 mL
Boiling water	2 cups	500 mL
Low-fat cottage cheese (less than 1% MF)	2 cups	500 mL
Skim milk	½ cup	125 mL
Lemon juice, fresh or bottled	2 tbsp.	30 mL
Canned chopped green chilies	4 oz.	114 mL
Salt	½ tsp.	2 mL
Pepper	⅛ tsp.	0.5 mL
Grated part-skim mozzarella cheese (35% less fat)	½ cup	125 mL
Grated low-fat sharp Cheddar cheese (less than 21 % MF)	½ cup	125 mL

Cook rice in water until tender and water is absorbed, about 15 minutes.

Smooth cottage cheese, milk and lemon juice in blender. Turn into bowl. Add rice.

Stir chilies, salt and pepper into rice.

Layer ½ rice mixture then ½ mozzarella cheese. Repeat. Bake, uncovered, in 350°F (175°C) oven for about 25 minutes.

Sprinkle with cheddar cheese. Bake 5 to 8 minutes more to melt. Makes 5½ cups (1.24 L).

NUTRITION GUIDE	½ cup (125 mL) contains:	
	Energy	240 Calories (1006 kJ)
	Cholesterol	17 mg
	Sodium	885 mg
	Fat	5.1 g

MUSHROOM CASSEROLE

Unusual and ever so tasty.

Fresh button mushrooms	**2 lbs.**	**900 g**
Lemon juice, fresh or bottled	**2 tbsp.**	**30 mL**
Salt	**$\frac{1}{2}$ tsp.**	**2 mL**
Pepper	**$\frac{1}{8}$ tsp.**	**0.5 mL**
Water	**$\frac{3}{4}$ cup**	**175 mL**
All-purpose flour	**3 tbsp.**	**50 mL**
Chicken bouillon powder (35% less salt)	**2 tsp.**	**10 mL**
Thyme	**$\frac{1}{8}$ tsp.**	**0.5 mL**
Pepper	**$\frac{1}{8}$ tsp.**	**0.5 mL**
Water	**$\frac{1}{4}$ cup**	**60 mL**
Evaporated skim milk	**$\frac{1}{2}$ cup**	**125 mL**
Sherry (or alcohol-free sherry)	**2 tbsp.**	**30 mL**

Place first 5 ingredients in large saucepan. Heat until it simmers. Cover. Simmer for about 10 minutes, stirring occasionally.

Mix flour, bouillon powder, thyme and pepper with second amount of water until no lumps remain. Stir into boiling mushroom mixture until it boils and thickens.

Add milk and sherry. Stir. Turn into 2 quart (2 L) casserole. Bake, uncovered, in 350°F (175°C) oven for 20 to 25 minutes. Makes 4 cups (900 mL).

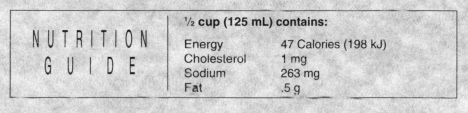

NUTRITION GUIDE	$\frac{1}{2}$ cup (125 mL) contains:	
	Energy	47 Calories (198 kJ)
	Cholesterol	1 mg
	Sodium	263 mg
	Fat	.5 g

Yes, postage is more expensive. But at least it sticks to one thing until it gets there.

BROCCOLI CASSEROLE

Colorful with its cheesy topping.

Chopped onion	1 cup	250 mL
Sliced fresh mushrooms	2 cups	500 mL
Water		
Frozen egg product, thawed (low-fat and cholesterol-free)	$\frac{1}{4}$ cup	60 mL
Egg white (large)	1	1
Salad dressing, page 98	$\frac{1}{4}$ cup	60 mL
Condensed cream of mushroom soup	10 oz.	284 mL
Salt	$\frac{1}{2}$ tsp.	2 mL
Pepper	$\frac{1}{8}$ tsp.	0.5 mL
Dry bread crumbs	$\frac{1}{3}$ cup	75 mL
Frozen chopped broccoli, thawed	2 × 10 oz.	2 × 284 g
Grated low-fat sharp Cheddar cheese (less than 21% MF)	1 cup	250 mL
Dry bread crumbs	$\frac{1}{3}$ cup	75 mL

Cook onion and mushrooms in some water for 20 to 30 minutes until tender. Drain.

In large bowl, spoon beat egg and egg white until mixed. Stir in next 6 ingredients. Add onion-mushroom mixture. Turn into 3 quart (3 L) casserole.

Mix cheese with remaining bread crumbs. Sprinkle over top. Cover. Bake in 350°F (175°C) oven for 35 minutes. Remove cover. Continue to bake about 10 minutes more until cheese melts. Makes $5\frac{2}{3}$ cups (1.28 L).

N U T R I T I O N G U I D E	$\frac{1}{2}$ cup (125 mL) contains:	
	Energy	137 Calories (580 kJ)
	Cholesterol	10 mg
	Sodium	551 mg
	Fat	5.8 g

GREEN BEAN CASSEROLE

The secret of the good flavor is the addition of soy sauce. Serve with hot rolls.

Chopped fresh mushrooms	2 cups	500 mL
Chopped onion	½ cup	125 mL
All-purpose flour	3 tbsp.	50 mL
Pepper	⅛ tsp.	0.5 mL
Skim milk	1½ cups	375 mL
Light soy sauce (40% less salt)	2 tbsp.	30 mL
Grated low-fat sharp Cheddar cheese (less than 21% MF)	1 cup	250 mL
Sliced water chestnuts, drained	5 oz.	142 mL
Frozen beans, cooked, whole, cut or French style	2 × 10 oz.	2 × 284 g
Sliced almonds, browned in 350°F (175°C) oven about 5 minutes	2 tbsp.	30 mL

Spray frying pan with no-stick cooking spray. Add mushrooms and onion. Sauté until soft.

Measure flour and pepper in bowl. Mix in a little milk until no lumps remain. Add rest of milk and soy sauce. Stir into mushroom mixture until it boils and thickens.

Stir in cheese, water chestnuts and beans. Turn into 2 quart (2 L) casserole.

Sprinkle with almonds. Bake, uncovered, in 350°F (175°C) oven for 30 minutes until bubbly hot. Makes 5¼ cups (1.18 L).

NUTRITION GUIDE	½ cup (125 mL) contains:	
	Energy	90 Calories (377 kJ)
	Cholesterol	7 mg
	Sodium	220 mg
	Fat	3.1 g

THREE CHEESE MANICOTTI

Shells are stuffed with a tasty filling covered with a meatless tomato sauce.

Manicotti shells	8	8
Boiling water	3 qts.	3 L

FILLING

Low-fat cottage cheese (less than 1% MF)	1½ cups	350 mL
Grated part-skim mozzarella cheese (35% less fat)	1 cup	250 mL
Grated Parmesan cheese	¼ cup	60 mL
Large egg	1	1
All-purpose flour	1 tbsp.	15 mL
Oregano	½ tsp.	2 mL
Chives	1 tbsp.	15 mL
Salt	¼ tsp.	1 mL
Pepper	⅛ tsp.	0.5 mL
Garlic powder	¼ tsp.	1 mL
Skim milk	3 tbsp.	50 mL

TOMATO SAUCE

Canned tomatoes, mashed	14 oz.	398 mL
Chopped onion	½ cup	125 mL
Chopped celery	¼ cup	50 mL
Granulated sugar	½ tsp.	2 mL
Parsley flakes	½ tsp.	2 mL
Salt	½ tsp.	2 mL
Pepper	⅛ tsp.	0.5 mL
Oregano	¼ tsp.	1 mL
Basil	¼ tsp.	1 mL
Garlic powder	¼ tsp.	1 mL

Cook manicotti in boiling water in large uncovered Dutch oven about 5 to 6 minutes until barely tender. Drain. Rinse with cold water. Drain.

Filling: Stir all ingredients in bowl in order given. Carefully stuff shells.

(continued on next page)

Tomato Sauce: Combine all ingredients in saucepan. Stir. Bring to a boil. Simmer, stirring occasionally about 20 minutes until liquid reduces. Pour about ⅓ sauce in 9 x 9 inch (22 x 22 cm) pan. Arrange manicotti over top in single layer. Cover with remaining sauce. Cover. Bake in 350°F (175°C) oven for about 40 minutes until hot and bubbly. Makes 8 manicotti.

N U T R I T I O N G U I D E	**1 manicotti contains:**	
	Energy	191 Calories (800 kJ)
	Cholesterol	40 mg
	Sodium	667 mg
	Fat	5 g

QUICK BAKED BEANS

Good flavor. Rich dark brown color. So easy.

Baked beans in tomato sauce	2 x 14 oz.	2 x 398 mL
Unsweetened crushed pineapple	1 cup	250 mL
Instant coffee granules	1 tsp.	5 mL
Prepared mustard	1 tsp.	5 mL
Liquid smoke	¼ tsp.	1 mL
Liquid sweetener	1 tsp.	5 mL
Chopped onion	½ cup	125 mL
Sliced fresh mushrooms	1 cup	250 mL
Diced green pepper (optional)	¼ cup	60 mL

Combine first 6 ingredients in bean pot or 1½ quart (1.5 L) casserole.

Spray frying pan with no-stick cooking spray. Add onion, mushrooms and green pepper. Sauté until soft. Add to bean mixture. Stir. Bake, uncovered, in 350°F (175°C) oven for about 1 hour until browned and bubbly. Makes 4¼ cups (950 mL).

N U T R I T I O N G U I D E	**½ cup (125 mL) contains:**	
	Energy	121 Calories (506 kJ)
	Cholesterol	0 mg
	Sodium	409 mg
	Fat	.6 g

TOMATO SCALLOP

An old,old recipe that is still good today. Quick and easy.

Canned tomatoes, broken up	28 oz.	796 mL
Dry bread crumbs	2⅓ cups	525 mL
Finely minced onion	1½ tbsp.	25 mL
Dry mustard	1 tsp.	5 mL
Granulated sugar	1 tsp.	5 mL
Salt	¼ tsp	1 mL
Pepper	¼ tsp.	1 mL
White bread slices (or brown)	2	2
Hard margarine, softened	2 tsp.	10 mL

Combine first 7 ingredients in 2 quart (2 L) casserole.

Spread bread thinly with margarine. Cut into cubes. Spread over tomatoes. Bake, uncovered, in 350°F (175°C) oven for about 30 minutes until bubbly. Makes 8 servings.

Pictured on page 107.

NUTRITION GUIDE	1 serving contains:	
	Energy	170 Calories (713 kJ)
	Cholesterol	1 mg
	Sodium	518 mg
	Fat	2.8 g

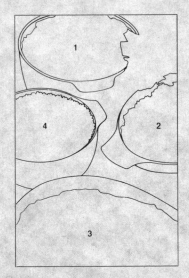

Casserole Dishes Courtesy Of:
The Bay China Dept.

Changes peas from ordinary to extraordinary.

Chopped onion	½ **cup**	**125 mL**
Boiling water		
Sliced fresh mushrooms	**1 cup**	**250 mL**
Frozen peas	**2 cups**	**500 mL**
CREAM SAUCE		
All-purpose flour	**4 tsp.**	**20 mL**
Skim milk	**1 cup**	**225 mL**
Salt	½ **tsp.**	**2 mL**
Pepper	⅛ **tsp.**	**0.5 mL**
Paprika	¼ **tsp.**	**1 mL**
Hard margarine	**1 tbsp.**	**15 mL**
Dry bread crumbs	¼ **cup**	**60 mL**

Cook onion in some boiling water until almost done.

Add mushrooms and peas. Cook for 3 to 4 minutes. Drain. Pour into 1 quart (1 L) casserole.

Cream Sauce: Place flour in small saucepan. Mix in a small amount of milk until no lumps remain. Add remaining milk, salt, pepper and paprika. Heat and stir until it boils and thickens slightly. Pour over vegetables. Stir lightly.

Melt margarine in small saucepan. Stir in bread crumbs. Sprinkle over top. Bake in 350°F (175°C) oven for 20 to 30 minutes until hot and browned lightly. Makes 2½ cups (575 mL).

Pictured on page 89.

N U T R I T I O N G U I D E	½ **cup (125 mL) contains:**	
	Energy	132 Calories (553 kJ)
	Cholesterol	1 mg
	Sodium	425 mg
	Fat	2.9 g

SCALLOPED POTATOES

Just good potatoes. Just a trace of fat.

All-purpose flour	¼ cup	60 mL
Dill weed	½ tsp.	2 mL
Salt	¾ tsp.	4 mL
Pepper	⅛ tsp.	0.5 mL
Skim milk	2 cups	500 mL
Medium potatoes, sliced ¼ inch (6 mm) thick	6	6
Large onion, thinly sliced	1	1

Stir flour, dill weed, salt and pepper together in saucepan. Mix in milk gradually until no lumps remain. Heat and stir until it boils and thickens. Remove from heat.

Place ½ potatoes and ½ onion in 2 quart (2 L) casserole. Pour ½ sauce over top. Repeat. Cover. Bake in 350°F (175°C) oven for about 1½ hours or until potatoes are tender. Remove cover for a few minutes to brown if desired. Makes 6 servings.

NUTRITION GUIDE	1 serving contains:	
	Energy	206 Calories (861 kJ)
	Cholesterol	2 mg
	Sodium	392 mg
	Fat	trace

Astronauts have their launch at noon.

An old-timer pared down to suit today's lifestyle.

Dry elbow macaroni	2 cups	500 mL
Boiling water	3 qts.	3 L
All-purpose flour	3½ tbsp.	50 mL
Salt	¾ tsp.	4 mL
Pepper	⅛ tsp.	0.5 mL
Paprika	¼ tsp.	1 mL
Skim milk	2⅓ cups	575 mL
Grated low-fat sharp Cheddar cheese (less than 21% MF)	1 cup	250 mL
Onion flakes	2 tbsp.	30 mL
Dry mustard	½ tsp.	2 mL
TOPPING		
Hard margarine	1 tbsp.	15 mL
Dry bread crumbs	⅓ cup	75 mL

Cook macaroni in boiling water in large uncovered pot about 5 to 7 minutes until tender but firm. Drain. Return macaroni to pot.

Stir flour, salt, pepper and paprika together in saucepan. Mix in part of the milk until no lumps remain. Add rest of milk. Heat and stir until it boils and thickens.

Add cheese, onion flakes and mustard. Stir well. Add to macaroni. Stir. Pour into 2 quart (2 L) casserole.

Topping: Melt margarine in small saucepan. Stir in bread crumbs. Sprinkle over top. Bake, uncovered, in 350°F (175°C) oven for about 30 minutes until hot and bubbly. Makes 6 cups (1.35 L).

NUTRITION GUIDE	1 cup (250 mL) contains:	
	Energy	298 Calories (1247 kJ)
	Cholesterol	14 mg
	Sodium	584 mg
	Fat	7.1 g

BARLEY BAKE

This makes a nice change from potatoes and rice.

Beef bouillon powder (35% less salt)	2 tbsp.	30 mL
Boiling water	3½ cups	875 mL
Barley, pot or pearl	1 cup	250 mL
Chopped onion	1½ cups	375 mL
Parsley flakes	2 tsp.	10 mL
Chopped green onions	¼ cup	60 mL
Pepper	¼ tsp.	1 mL
Pine nuts or slivered almonds, browned in 350°F (175°C) oven for about 5 minutes, for garnish	2 tsp.	10 mL

Stir bouillon powder into water in 2 quart (2 L) casserole.

Add next 5 ingredients.

Garnish with pine nuts. Cover. Bake in 350°F (175°C) oven for about 2 hours until barley is tender. Makes about 4¼ cups (950 mL).

Pictured on page 143.

NUTRITION GUIDE	½ cup (125 mL) contains:	
	Energy	79 Calories (329 kJ)
	Cholesterol	trace
	Sodium	207 mg
	Fat	3.4 g

CAULIFLOWER-BROCCOLI CASSEROLE

Fast and easy. Vegetables are used in the frozen state. Good.

Frozen cauliflower	10 oz.	284 g
Frozen broccoli	10 oz.	284 g
Finely chopped onion	⅓ cup	75 mL
Condensed cream of mushroom soup	10 oz.	284 mL
Grated low-fat sharp Cheddar cheese (less than 21% MF)	⅓ cup	75 mL
Corn flake crumbs	¼ cup	60 mL

(continued on next page)

Layer cauliflower, broccoli and onion in 2 quart (2 L) casserole. Cut large chunks with sharp knife.

Place soup in bowl. Add cheese. Stir. Spoon over casserole.

Sprinkle with corn flake crumbs. Bake, uncovered, in 350°F (175°C) oven for about 60 minutes. Makes 3½ cups (800 mL).

Pictured on page 53.

NUTRITION GUIDE	½ cup (125 mL) contains:	
	Energy	95 Calories (397 kJ)
	Cholesterol	3 mg
	Sodium	432 mg
	Fat	4.4 g

LUNCH SPECIAL

Begin with a convenience food, add vegetables and you have a quick, easy luncheon dish.

Packaged macaroni and cheese dinner	7¼ oz.	200 g
Sliced fresh mushrooms	1½ cups	375 mL
Skim milk	⅓ cup	75 mL
All-purpose flour	⅓ cup	75 mL
Chicken bouillon powder (35% less salt)	1 tsp.	5 mL
Paprika	⅛ tsp.	0.5 mL
Cayenne pepper	⅛ tsp.	0.5 mL
Skim milk	1 cup	250 mL
Peas, fresh or frozen, cooked	1 cup	250 mL

Salt and pepper to taste

Prepare macaroni according to directions on package, omitting salt and margarine or butter and adding mushrooms to macaroni to cook at the same time. Drain. Stir in cheese packet and milk.

Whisk first amount of milk with flour in saucepan until smooth. Add bouillon powder, paprika and cayenne pepper. Add second amount of milk. Heat and stir until it boils and thickens. Add to macaroni mixture.

Add peas. Stir. Turn into 2 quart (2 L) casserole. Bake, uncovered, in 350°F (175°C) oven for 20 to 30 minutes. Makes 5⅓ cups (1.2 L).

NUTRITION GUIDE	1 cup (225 mL) contains:	
	Energy	271 Calories (1132 kJ)
	Cholesterol	7.4 mg
	Sodium	298 mg
	Fat	3.6 g

GREEN CHILI QUICHE

Wedges are topped with green and yellow. Easy.

Unbaked 9 inch (22 cm) pastry shell, page 104	1	1
Grated part-skim mozzarella cheese (35% less fat)	1½ cups	350 mL
Grated low-fat sharp Cheddar cheese (less than 21% MF)	½ cup	125 mL
Canned chopped green chilies	4 oz.	114 mL
Egg white (large)	1	1
Frozen egg product, thawed (low-fat and cholesterol-free)	½ cup	125 mL
All-purpose flour	2 tbsp.	30 mL
Salt	¼ tsp.	1 mL
Cumin	¼ tsp.	1 mL
Evaporated skim milk	1 cup	250 mL

Prepare pastry shell. Do not prick.

Sprinkle next 3 ingredients in layers in pastry shell.

Mix egg white, egg product, flour, salt and cumin in bowl. Add milk. Stir. Pour over top. Bake in 350°F (175°C) oven for about 40 minutes until set. Freezes well. Makes 8 servings.

Pictured on page 107.

NUTRITION GUIDE	1 serving contains:	
	Energy	245 Calories (1024 kJ)
	Cholesterol	18 mg
	Sodium	490 mg
	Fat	12 g

Variation: May be baked in a pie plate without pastry shell. Spray pie plate with no-stick cooking spray. One serving will contain only 5 g of fat.

A foot is a great device for finding furniture in the dark.

This economical vegetable is transformed.

Head of cabbage, cut in 6 wedges, core intact	**1½ lbs.**	**800 g**
Boiling water		
All-purpose flour	**¼ cup**	**60 mL**
Salt	**¾ tsp.**	**4 mL**
Pepper	**¼ tsp.**	**1 mL**
Garlic powder	**⅛ tsp.**	**0.5 mL**
Onion powder	**⅛ tsp.**	**0.5 mL**
Skim milk	**2 cups**	**500 mL**
Grated low-fat sharp Cheddar cheese (less than 21 % MF)	**½ cup**	**125 mL**
Grated low-fat sharp Cheddar cheese (less than 21 % MF)	**½ cup**	**125 mL**

Cook cabbage in some boiling water for about 10 minutes until tender. Using slotted spoon, lift out wedges as best you can and place in 3 quart (3 L) casserole. Pile loose leaves on top.

Measure next 5 ingredients into saucepan. Mix in part of milk until no lumps remain. Add rest of milk. Heat and stir until it boils and thickens.

Stir in first amount of cheese. Pour over cabbage.

Sprinkle with remaining cheese. Cover. Bake in 350°F (175°C) oven for 20 to 30 minutes until hot. Makes 6 servings.

Pictured on page 143.

NUTRITION GUIDE	1 serving contains:	
	Energy	155 Calories (647 kJ)
	Cholesterol	14 mg
	Sodium	551 mg
	Fat	4.7 g

METRIC CONVERSION

Throughout this book measurements are given in Conventional and Metric measure. To compensate for differences between the two measurements due to rounding, a full metric measure is not always used. The cup used is the standard 8 fluid ounce. Temperature is given in degrees Fahrenheit and Celsius. Baking pan measurements are in inches and centimetres as well as quarts and litres. An exact metric conversion is given below as well as the working equivalent (Standard Measure).

OVEN TEMPERATURES

Fahrenheit (°F)	Celsius (°C)
175°	80°
200°	95°
225°	110°
250°	120°
275°	140°
300°	150°
325°	160°
350°	175°
375°	190°
400°	205°
425°	220°
450°	230°
475°	240°
500°	260°

SPOONS

Conventional Measure	Metric Exact Conversion Millilitre (mL)	Metric Standard Measure Millilitre (mL)
1/4 teaspoon (tsp.)	1.2 mL	1 mL
1/2 teaspoon (tsp.)	2.4 mL	2 mL
1 teaspoon (tsp.)	4.7 mL	5 mL
2 teaspoons (tsp.)	9.4 mL	10 mL
1 tablespoon (tbsp.)	14.2 mL	15 mL

CUPS

1/4 cup (4 tbsp.)	56.8 mL	50 mL
1/3 cup (5 1/3 tbsp.)	75.6 mL	75 mL
1/2 cup (8 tbsp.)	113.7 mL	125 mL
2/3 cup (10 2/3 tbsp.)	151.2 mL	150 mL
3/4 cup (12 tbsp.)	170.5 mL	175 mL
1 cup (16 tbsp.)	227.3 mL	250 mL
4 1/2 cups	1022.9 mL	1000 mL (1 L)

DRY MEASUREMENTS

Ounces (oz.)	Grams (g)	Grams (g)
1 oz.	28.3 g	30 g
2 oz.	56.7 g	55 g
3 oz.	85.0 g	85 g
4 oz.	113.4 g	125 g
5 oz.	141.7 g	140 g
6 oz.	170.1 g	170 g
7 oz.	198.4 g	200 g
8 oz.	226.8 g	250 g
16 oz.	453.6 g	500 g
32 oz.	907.2 g	1000 g (1 kg)

PANS, CASSEROLES

Conventional Inches	Metric Centimetres	Conventional Quart (qt.)	Metric Litre (L)
8x8 inch	20x20 cm	1 2/3 qt.	2 L
9x9 inch	22x22 cm	2 qt.	2.5 L
9x13 inch	22x33 cm	3 1/3 qt.	4 L
10x15 inch	25x38 cm	1 qt.	1.2 L
11x17 inch	28x43 cm	1 1/4 qt.	1.5 L
8x2 inch round	20x5 cm	1 2/3 qt.	2 L
9x2 inch round	22x5 cm	2 qt.	2.5 L
10x4 1/2 inch tube	25x11 cm	4 1/4 qt.	5 L
8x4x3 inch loaf	20x10x7 cm	1 1/4 qt.	1.5 L
9x5x3 inch loaf	23x12x7 cm	1 2/3 qt.	2 L

INDEX

If you don't see Company's Coming where you shop, ask your retailer to give us a call. Meanwhile, we offer a mail order service for your convenience.

Just indicate the books you would like below. Then complete the reverse page and send your order with payment to us.

Buying a gift? Enclose a personal note or card and we will be pleased to send it with your order.

Deduct $5.00 for every $35.00 ordered.

See reverse.

Company's Coming COOKBOOKS

Company's Coming Publishing Limited
Box 8037, Station F
Edmonton, Alberta, Canada T6H 4N9
Tel: (403) 450-6223

MAIL ORDER COUPON

QUANTITY • HARD COVER BOOK •

Jean Paré's Favorites - Volume One

	TOTAL BOOKS	TOTAL PRICE
TOTAL $17.95 + $1.50 shipping = **$19.45 each** x Canadian residents include G.S.T. (see reverse)		= $

QUANTITY • SOFT COVER BOOKS •

ENGLISH

150 Delicious Squares	Pasta
Casseroles	Cakes
Muffins & More	Barbecues
Salads	Dinners of the World
Appetizers	Lunches
Desserts	Pies
Soups & Sandwiches	Light Recipes
Holiday Entertaining	Microwave Cooking
Cookies	Preserves
Vegetables	Light Casseroles
Main Courses	Chicken, Etc. (Apr. 1995)

	TOTAL BOOKS	TOTAL PRICE
TOTAL $10.95 + $1.50 shipping = **$12.45 each** x Canadian residents include G.S.T. (see reverse)		= $

QUANTITY • PINT SIZE BOOKS (SOFT COVER) •

Finger Food	Buffets
Party Planning	Baking Delights (Nov. 1994)

	TOTAL BOOKS	TOTAL PRICE
TOTAL $4.99 + $1.00 shipping = **$5.99 each** x Canadian residents include G.S.T. (see reverse)		= $

QUANTITY • SOFT COVER BOOKS •

FRENCH

150 délicieux carrés	Recettes légères
Les casseroles	Les salades
Muffins et plus	La cuisson au micro-ondes
Les dîners	Les pâtes
Les barbecues	Les conserves
Les tartes	Les casseroles légères
Délices des fêtes	Poulet, etc. (avr. 1995)

	TOTAL BOOKS	TOTAL PRICE
TOTAL $10.95 + $1.50 shipping = **$12.45 each** x Canadian residents include G.S.T. (see reverse)		= $

TOTAL PRICE FOR ALL BOOKS Canadian residents include G.S.T. (see reverse)	$

* *Please fill in reverse side of this coupon* *

Deduct $5.00 for every $35.00 ordered.

COOKBOOKS

Company's Coming Publishing Limited
Box 8037, Station F
Edmonton, Alberta, Canada T6H 4N9
Tel: (403) 450-6223

MAIL ORDER COUPON

TOTAL PRICE FOR ALL BOOKS (from reverse)	$
Less $5.00 for every $35.00 ordered	− $
SUBTOTAL	$
Canadian residents add G.S.T.	+ $
TOTAL AMOUNT ENCLOSED	$

• **MAKE CHEQUE OR MONEY ORDER PAYABLE TO:**
  COMPANY'S COMING PUBLISHING LIMITED

• **ORDERS OUTSIDE CANADA:**
  Must be paid in U.S. funds by cheque or money order drawn on Canadian or U.S. bank.

• *Prices subject to change without prior notice.*

• *Sorry, no C.O.D.'s*

Gift Giving

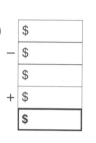

• Let us help you with your gift giving!
• We will send cookbooks directly to the recipients of your choice if you give us their names and addresses.
• Be sure to specify the titles of the cookbooks you wish to send to each person.
• If you would like to enclose your personal note or card, we will be pleased to include it with your gift order.

GIFT SHIPPING ADDRESS

Send my gift of Company's Coming Cookbooks listed on the reverse side of this coupon, to:

Name:

Street:

City: Province/State:

Postal Code/Zip: Tel: (   ) —

Company's Coming Cookbooks make excellent gifts. Birthdays, bridal showers, Mother's Day, Father's Day, graduation or any occasion... collect them all! Remember to enclose your personal note or card and we will be pleased to send it with your order.